Edith Wharton's
Prisoners
of Consciousness

Recent Titles in
Contributions in Women's Studies

Women, Men and Time: Gender Differences in Pail Work, Housework and Leisure
Beth Anne Shelton

Black Women in the Workplace: Impacts of Structural Change in the Economy
Bette Woody

Assertive Biblical Women
William E. Phipps

Seeking Common Ground: Multidisciplinary Studies of Immigrant Women in
the United States
Donna Gabaccia, editor

Clean Maids, True Wives, Steadfast Widows: Chaucer's Women
and Medieval Codes of Conduct
Margaret Hallissy

Style and the "Scribbling Women": An Empirical Analysis of Nineteenth-Century
American Fiction
Mary P. Hiatt

Refusal and Transgression in Joyce Carol Oates' Fiction
Marilyn C. Wesley

Becoming, Being, Bonding: Contemporary Feminism and Popular
Fiction by American Women Writers
Katherine B. Payant

Women's Lives and Public Policy: The International Experience
Meredeth Turshen and Briavel Holcomb, editors

Sex, Abortion and Unmarried Women
Paul Sachdev

Mules and Dragons: Popular Culture Images in the Selected Writings of African-
American and Chinese-American Women Writers
Mary E. Young

Women, Community, and the Hormel Strike of 1985–86
Neala J. Schleuning

Edith Wharton's Prisoners of Consciousness

A STUDY OF THEME AND TECHNIQUE IN THE TALES

Evelyn E. Fracasso

Contributions in Women's Studies, Number 140

GREENWOOD PRESS
Westport, Connecticut • London

Library of Congress Cataloging-in-Publication Data

Fracasso, Evelyn E.
    Edith Wharton's prisoners of consciousness : a study of theme and
technique in the tales / Evelyn E. Fracasso.
       p.   cm. — (Contributions in women's studies, ISSN 0147–104X ;
no. 140)
    Includes bibliographical references and index.
    ISBN 0–313–29155–1
    1. Wharton, Edith, 1862–1937—Criticism and interpretation.
2. Women and literature–United States. 3. Imprisonment in
literature. 4. Prisoners in literature.   I. Title.   II. Series.
PS3545.H16Z648   1994
813'.52—dc20   93–35841

British Library Cataloguing in Publication Data is available.

Library of Congress Catalog Card Number: 93–35841
ISBN: 0–313–29155–1
ISSN: 0147–104X

First published in 1994

Greenwood Press, 88 Post Road West, Westport, CT 06881
An imprint of Greenwood Publishing Group, Inc.

Printed in the United States of America

The paper used in this book complies with the
Permanent Paper Standard issued by the National
Information Standards Organization (Z39.48–1984).

10 9 8 7 6 5 4 3 2 1

Copyright Acknowledgments

For Bob
You changed my mourning into dancing.
Psalm 30:11

Contents

Preface

In the summer of 1986, I came upon R.W.B. Lewis's two-volume edition of Edith Wharton's short stories in the Quinnipiac College Library. I read each of them with delight—even those that critics have deemed inferior. At that time there was no critical text devoted to Wharton's short stories (Barbara A. White's *Edith Wharton: A Study of the Short Fiction* was not published until 1991) and certainly no comprehensive examination of the techniques she employs in her stories. This study, therefore, concentrates on Wharton's narrative art and its application to the theme of imprisonment in her tales. It shows, too, that Wharton, as Lewis notes in the "Preface" to his biography of Wharton, "took to drawing upon her writings *for* her writings" (xiv).

I am deeply indebted to a number of people for their help with this study. I want to express my gratitude to Professor Gale C. Schricker of Fordham University for her guidance and encouragement. I also owe a debt of gratitude to several of my Quinnipiac College colleagues: the library staff, in particular, Ellen Kissner, Margot Roten, and Janet Valeski for securing materials; the Computer Center staff, especially Janice Esposito and Peter DiDomenico for help with the computer; and the Faculty Research Committee, chaired by Linda Broker, for granting released time from my teaching.

Thanks are also due the Watkins/Loomis Agency, Inc.; Charles Scribner's Sons, an imprint of Macmillan Publishing Company; the Yale Collection of

American Literature, Beinecke Rare Book and Manuscript Library, Yale University; and William Royall Tyler for permission to quote from Wharton's works and letters. The editors of the *College Language Association Journal* and the *Journal of the Short Story in English* also granted permission to use material in Chapters 2 and 3 that originally appeared in these journals.

Lastly, I wish to extend a special thank you to my children and their spouses—Mark and Michele, Paula and John, Robert, Maria, and Peter—for their love and support.

Chapter One

Introduction to Wharton's Theme and Technique

In her autobiography, *A Backward Glance*, Edith Wharton reveals: "The imagining of tales (about grown-up people, 'real people,' I called them—children always seemed to me incompletely realized) had gone on in me since my first conscious moments; I cannot remember the time when I did not want to 'make up' stories (33). She even recalls occasions when as a child she abandoned invited guests, imploring her mother to entertain them because she had to "*make up*" (35). It is not surprising, therefore, that years later, in a letter to Judge Robert Grant, Wharton acknowledged a feeling of superiority in the short story form:

> As soon as I look at a subject from the novel-angle I see it in its relation to a larger whole, in all its remotest connotations; & I can't help trying to take them in, at the cost of the smaller realism that I arrive at, I think, better in my short stories. This is the reason why I have always obscurely felt that I didn't know how to write a novel. I feel it more clearly after each attempt, because it is in such sharp contrast to the sense of authority with which I take hold of a short story.

This "sense of authority" spanned Wharton's entire lifetime, enabling her to produce, in addition to her many novels, novellas, poetry, and other miscellaneous works, eleven volumes of eighty-six short stories that span the beginning and the end of her completed published work.

All of these stories involve "real people," as Wharton calls them, their "looks and ways and words" (*BG* 211–12),[1] and especially their anxieties, their pain, and their suffering. For Edith Wharton believed that real people lead sad lives. "Life is the saddest thing there is, next to death" (*BG* 379), she tells us, and her stories reflect that sadness. Hers are not romantic narratives. She never cared for fairy tales, the fabulous, or the legendary (*BG* 4), and, consequently, her tales, with few exceptions, depict heroes and heroines leading unhappy lives. "There is a flavor of profound tragedy in all her work," H. Wayne Morgan maintains, "a belief that man is the victim of circumstances in life not entirely of his own making and beyond his control" (35). Similarly, Marius Bewley speaks of the protagonists in Wharton's fiction as "hopelessly trapped by the demands or the refusal of their society, or by the vacuity of their social aspirations, or by the various deprivations imposed on them by life" (147), and James E. Miller, Jr., points out that in Wharton's novels "her obsessive theme is that of the trapped sensibility" (85).

To provide thematic emphasis in her stories for these trapped victims of fate, Wharton made extravagant use of the enclosed space, especially the prison cell. It was an image not unfamiliar to her in her own life. In a letter to her close friend, Sara Norton, shortly after the publication of *The House of Mirth*, she writes, "And how I understand that love of living, of being in this wonderful, astounding world, even if one can look at it only through the prison bars of illness & suffering!" R.W.B. Lewis, in *Edith Wharton: A Biography*, points out that Wharton used the prison cell, "the most fearful of shut-in spaces—as the image of a number of her characters' condition in life, and by implication of her personal state" (121). Gary H. Lindberg, in his critical study *Edith Wharton and the Novel of Manners*, elaborates further on Wharton's symbolic use of the prison cell:

> Society functions as a prison in her fiction, not because the individual, "trailing clouds of glory," has accidentally fallen into it, nor because he is being tested by exposure to its confines, but because he has been born and reared in it; he learns to perceive reality through the bars of a cage. (36)

Clearly, the metaphor of life as prison obsessed Wharton, and, consequently, it appears in most of her short stories.

In her earliest tales (1891–1904), however, allusions to the prison image are for the most part indirect. In her first story, "Mrs. Manstey's View"

---

1. All parenthetical references to Edith Wharton's *A Backward Glance* in this study are abbreviated *BG*.

(1891), for example, a widow confined to the third-floor back room of a New York boardinghouse spends her days looking out the window at the life below. When she discovers that an addition on the house next door will soon obstruct her view, she decides to unlock the door to her apartment and the "iron door" (1:10) of the basement, both doors symbolic of her prisonlike existence, in order to burn down this "barrier of brick and mortar" (1: 6).[2] In "That Good May Come" (1894), a tale written a few years later, Maurice Birkton, a fledgling poet, prostitutes his art by selling a scandalous squib and shuts himself in his room where, imprisoned with guilt, he stirs uneasily "with the thwarted movements of a caged animal" (1: 40). A year later, in "The Lamp of Psyche" (1895), Delia Corbett, an ecstatic bride of two months, basks in the "imprisoned sunlight" (1:46) of her "most admirable" (1: 44) husband's library, only to wallow later in the imprisoned enlightenment of his not-so-admirable flaws.

In the stories written during Wharton's major phase (1905–1919), references to imprisonment become increasingly more explicit. In "The Triumph of Night" (1914), for example, Frank Rainer, a sickly young man of wealth, is being manipulated by his avaricious though ostensibly solicitous uncle and speaks in a "sad imprisoned voice" (2: 331) as he signs his will leaving millions to his uncle. In "Autres Temps . . . " (1911), Mrs. Lidcote, a middle-aged divorcée, continues to be ostracized by the New York society that unhesitatingly accepts her daughter's recent divorce and moans:

> "We're all imprisoned, of course—all of us middling people, who don't carry our freedom in our brains. But we've accommodated ourselves to our different cells, and if we're moved suddenly into the new ones we're likely to find a stone wall where we thought there was thin air, and to knock ourselves senseless against it." (2: 279)

Likewise, in "The Bolted Door" (1909), Hubert Granice, an unsuccessful middle-aged writer who murdered his wealthy cousin for his inheritance ten years ago, now begins to feel that he is

> chained to life—a "prisoner of consciousness." Where was it he had read the phrase? Well, he was learning what it meant. In the long night hours, when his brain seemed ablaze, he was visited by a sense of his fixed identity, of his irreducible, inexpugnable *selfness*, keener, more insidious, more unescapable, than any sensation he had ever known. He had not guessed that the mind

---

2. All parenthetical references to Edith Wharton's stories in this study are from R.W.B. Lewis's two-volume work, *The Collected Short Stories of Edith Wharton*.

was capable of such intricacies of self-realization, of penetrating so deep into
its own dark windings. (2: 23)

In the stories written during Wharton's late period (1926–1937), references to imprisonment continue to occur. In "The Day of the Funeral"
(1933), for example, Ambrose Trenham, a university professor whose wife
committed suicide because of his adulterous conduct, returns to his house
the night of the funeral after a final meeting with his mistress, bars the door,
and listens "to that familiar slipping of the bolts and clink of the chain" (2:
686). In "Confession" (1936), Kate Spain, the daughter of a wealthy and
tyrannical father, left "the prison of her father's house" (2: 813) only to
suffer another prisonlike existence shunning the notoriety following his
murder. In "All Souls' " (1937), Sara Clayburn, a resolute fifty-year-old
widow, breaks her ankle in a deserted, isolated old house on a snowy Sunday
in November, and she begins to feel that she is a "prisoner" (2: 888) of
silence and fear, "the fear that she might lie there alone and untended till
she died of cold, and of the terror of her solitude" (2: 890).

Hence, Wharton's tragic victims are prisoners of consciousness because
of their marital state, the dictates of society, their moral choices as artists,
or their fear of the supernatural. Some attempt an unsuccessful escape from
their imprisoned state, some remain resigned, a few are able to liberate
themselves from their imprisonment, but most endure a death-in-life existence.

In the last several decades, critical studies of Wharton's fiction have
focused on her theme of imprisonment, but invariably it is related to
biographical considerations. Admittedly, Edith Wharton's unsuccessful
marriage to Edward Robbins ("Teddy") Wharton, her love affair with
Morton Fullerton, and her close relationship with Walter Berry contributed
to the thematic emphasis in her shorter works. However, this study is not
concerned with such insights and influences; rather it concentrates on the
development of Wharton's technical artistry in presenting her imprisonment
theme.

Technique was essential to Wharton. Without it, she argues, "pure anar-
chy in fiction," or "formlessness," results (*WF* 14).[3] In *A Backward Glance*,
she notes that there are two parts to the storytelling process: "that which
concerns the technique of fiction (in the widest sense), and that which tries
to look into what, for want of a simpler term, one must call by the old bardic
name of inspiration" (199). Similarly, in *The Writing of Fiction*, Wharton

maintains that "the effect produced by the short story depends almost entirely on its form, or presentation" (48). She even defines exactly what she means by "form" and "style":

> Form might perhaps, for present purposes, be defined as the order, in time and importance, in which the incidents of the narrative are grouped; and style as the way in which they are presented, not only in the narrower sense of language, but also, and rather, as they are grasped and coloured by their medium, the narrator's mind, and given back in his words. (*WF* 23–24)

Wharton concluded, therefore, that form and style are "inextricably interwoven" with the matter of subject and that both ought "to spring naturally out of the particular theme chosen for representation" (*WF* 23).

Consequently, from the beginning of her short story writing, Wharton experimented with a variety of stylistic devices in order to provide thematic definition—in structure with tantalizing beginnings, surprise endings, framing, and flashbacks; in language with dialogue, interior monologues, irony, and satire (at which she became a master); in setting with symbolic imagery; in point of view with first-person and omniscient narrators.

In *The Writing of Fiction*, Wharton discusses many of these techniques, techniques that provide the basis for this study. She believed, for example, that the first page of the short story should contain "the germ of the whole" and that "the writer's first care should be to know how to make a beginning" (50–51). In short, the "attack," as she calls it, should be "the short-story writer's first concern, once he has mastered his subject" (51). This principle governs the beginnings of all her stories, but perhaps none more dramatically than her ghost story "Afterward" (1910). In the first lines of the tale, uttered to Ned and Mary Boyne, an American couple seeking to escape their dreary existence in a Midwest mining town by renting an old "uncomfortable" house in England where they can enjoy writing and painting, Wharton plants her first seeds of meaning: "Oh, there *is* one [a ghost], of course, but you'll never know it. . . . Not till long long afterward" (2: 152–53). The phrase "not till long afterward" recurs throughout the narrative whenever Mary sees shadows and elusive figures, but it is not until the final lines of the tale, when she realizes the identity of the mysterious stranger who disappeared with her husband, that its meaning finally becomes clear. For the last time, she hears the haunting words that contain "the germ of the whole": "You won't know till afterward. . . . You won't know till long, long afterward" (2: 176).

However, Wharton did not rely only on dramatic openings to reveal meaning in her tales. She tells us that throughout the entire narrative there should be a gradual unfolding of the "*illuminating incident*" to reveal "the inner meaning of each situation" (*WF* 109) and, by implication, the meaning of the entire story. In "The Seed of Faith" (1918), Willard Bent, a missionary in Morocco, prays at the beginning of the tale for "a sign" (2: 421) that will give meaning to his life. At the end of the narrative, when his superior seizes the Koran from the Mosque and urges Bent to pray for strength, such a sign does appear. The phrase "*Say among the heathen that the Lord reigneth*" suddenly flashes before him "in letters of fire" (2: 446), impelling him to spit upon and trample the Koran—the only decisive step he takes against the heathen Moslems. This flashing phrase clarifies the sign "cast forward from the first page" (*WF* 110) and is as meaningful as the dramatic opening of "Afterward."

The endings of her stories also concerned Wharton, and she cautions that an "unreal ending diminishes the short tale in value" (*WF* 50). However, she was not averse to the surprise ending, and in fact, many of her stories do conclude with an unexpected, albeit realistic, twist. In "The Potboiler" (1904), Ned Stanwell, an idealistic young painter, sacrifices his artistic convictions by painting the portrait of a society matron in order to earn money to win Kate Arran, the poverty-stricken woman he loves. At the conclusion of the narrative, Kate informs him, much to his dismay, that she has already agreed to marry Mungold, the well-to-do fashionable painter of the day, "because, though his pictures are bad, he does not prostitute his art" (1: 684). The ending, though unexpected, is not unrealistic.

Wharton also articulates several principles with regard to language throughout *The Writing of Fiction*. She believes that "words are the exterior symbols of thought, and it is only by their exact use that the writer can keep on his subject" (24). Therefore, she maintains that "every word, every stroke, tells" (114) and that "every phrase should be a sign-post, and never (unless intentionally) a misleading one" (37). In "Permanent Wave" (1935), one of her last tales, the phrase "late as usual" (2: 789), introduced as the story opens, is one of Wharton's intentionally misleading "sign-posts." Nalda Craig, the unhappily married wife of a self-centered economist, is painfully aware that she is invariably late for all her engagements and appointments. Consequently, when she is told that it is a day later than she thinks, she mistakenly believes she has missed the flight to Central America with her lover, a charming and exciting explorer. Allusions to time and to Nalda's customary tardiness pervade the narrative, until, at its conclusion, she hysterically discovers that she was misinformed. Instead of being "late as usual," she is, in fact, early. This misleading "sign-post" introduced at the beginning of the tale demonstrates Wharton at her ironic best.

Perhaps Wharton had more to say about dialogue than any other aspect of language because, she tells us in *A Backward Glance*, she attaches much importance to dialogue (203). However, she feels that it should be "sparingly used" and that it should "record only the significant passages of their [her characters'] talk, in high relief against the narrative, and not uselessly embedded in it" (203). Likewise, in *The Writing of Fiction*, Wharton suggests that dialogue be reserved for "culminating moments" (73). In "Duration" (1936), another tale from her late period, the dialogue of Martha Little, a feisty spinster celebrating her one-hundredth birthday, is minimal. However, Miss Little's attitude toward Syngleton Perch, the great-uncle claiming that he is also a centenarian so that he can share her town-wide birthday festivities, becomes quite clear from their brief, caustic exchanges. Martha Little addresses Uncle Syngleton only three times in the narrative: she resentfully rebukes him for his belated announcement of his centenarian status, she belligerently orders him to "keep going!" (2: 869) when she sees him at her celebration rehearsal, and she cunningly asks him to assist her to her seat on the platform so that she can trip him with her cane and rob him of sharing her spotlight. All of Miss Little's comments are revealing; all signal "culminating moments."

Moreover, Wharton believed that character and setting are intimately related to each other. She argues that the effect produced by scenic detail should always "be an event in the history of a soul, and the use of the 'descriptive passage,' and its style, should be determined by the fact that it must depict only what the intelligence concerned would have noticed, and always in terms within the register of that intelligence" (*WF* 85). Consequently, she frequently made use of symbolic settings to reflect her central characters' thoughts and feelings. In "Friends" (1900), one of Wharton's early tales, Penelope Bent, a middle-aged spinster, returns to her hometown after having been jilted by a scoundrel who married another. Embarrassed and ashamed, she veils her face as she walks through the streets of the town so that she will not be recognized. The narrative begins with a scenic description of the town that mirrors Penelope's despondent state: "Sailport is an ugly town. . . . The streets, too narrow for the present needs of the town, run between buildings of discordant character . . . full of snow and mud in winter, of dust and garbage in summer. . . . Nowhere is there the least peep of green" (1: 197). Each detail depicts only what Penelope notices; each reflects her feelings of humiliation and shame.

Point of view was of particular interest to Wharton, and she remarks early in *The Writing of Fiction* that "the short-story writer must not only know from what angle to present his anecdote if it is to give out all its fires, but must understand just *why* that particular angle and no other is the right one"

(*WF* 48–49). In "The Moving Finger" (1901), Wharton shifts the angle three times in order to achieve just the "right one." She begins with an author-observer who provides background information about Ralph Grancy, an international diplomat who commissions a portrait of his beautiful second wife; she later shifts to Grancy, who reveals why he wants the painting aged; and she concludes with the portrait painter, who explains why he has restored the painting to its original condition. Each angle is necessary for a complete understanding of the narrative; each is essential "to give out all its fires."

In a number of her short stories, Wharton enhanced the particular angle from which the story is told with the stream of consciousness technique. Although she decried its use, contending that it records an "unsorted abundance" of irrelevant reactions, she nonetheless employed this artistic device in order to set down "mental as well as visual reactions . . . just as they come" (*WF* 12). In "Joy in the House" (1933), a story from her late period, Wharton records both the mental and visual reactions of Christine Ansley, a discontented wife and mother who returns to her wealthy, self-centered husband after a six-month affair with a struggling, impoverished artist. From the beginning of the tale, when she realizes that her affair was a mistake—"Yes; she saw it now" (2: 710)—to her arrival home—"It was soothing to move from one tidy room to the other, noting that ash trays and paper baskets had been emptied, cushions shaken up, scattered newspapers banished" (2: 717)—to her discovery that her husband has withheld the news of her lover's suicide—"She must get away, get away at once from this stifling atmosphere of tolerance and benevolence, of smoothing over and ignoring and dissembling" (2: 721)—all of Christine's responses are set down "just as they come."

Literary critics have written about many of the techniques that Wharton discusses. They note especially her "magnificent phrasing," which unobtrusively fits her theme (Quinn 580), her "skillful use of dialogue" (Plante 365), her "extraordinary sensitiveness to the local features of landscape and architecture" (Nevius 44), and her irony, which ranges "from the straight satirical to the almost tragic" (Walton 111). Although these critics make mention of some aspect of Wharton's craft, they fail to present a comprehensive examination of the techniques in her short stories.

This study, therefore, concentrates on Wharton's skill as a craftsman, in consciously and carefully fitting her narrative techniques to the theme of imprisonment. It shows that the theme of imprisonment was not just transposed from life to work but was fully integrated with her artistic techniques. It examines, through close textual analysis, a number of representative tales from Wharton's early period (1891–1904), her major phase

(1905–1919), and her later years (1926–1937). These tales are divided into four categories based on the different types of imprisonment that Wharton's tragic heroes and heroines experience. Frances Theresa Russell contends that "Edith Wharton's first concern is with individuals, her second with people in the lump called 'society,' and her last with the entire aggregation known as humanity" ("Imagery" 457). The categories of imprisonment in this study are arranged to correspond to these concerns: individuals trapped by love and marriage are discussed in Chapter 2, men and women imprisoned by the dictates of society in Chapter 3, human beings victimized by the demands of art and morality in Chapter 4. An additional category, persons paralyzed by fear of the supernatural, is examined in Chapter 5, because of the number of ghost stories Wharton wrote involving the imprisonment theme. Chapter 6 concludes the study with a review of Wharton's thematic and technical development from her early to her later tales.

Selection of the tales in these four categories is based on two considerations. Lewis, in the Preface to his biography of Wharton, notes that "she took to drawing upon her writings *for* her writings, creating new novels in part out of the emotional and psychological ingredients of old novels or unfinished fragments of novels" (xiv). This observation certainly applies to her tales. Many of Wharton's later stories are latent in those written at the beginning of her career. Therefore, tales that contain similar subject matter, and often parallel story lines, have been selected from Wharton's early period and compared to those written in her major and late periods in order to point out the development of her theme and technique. Furthermore, most of the stories selected for this study have had little or no analysis by Wharton critics. Only a few familiar tales are included because they clearly illustrate Wharton's innovative use of a wide variety of stylistic devices. It is an area too long overlooked despite the fact that so many of her critics single out this magnificent aspect of her work. Fred Lewis Pattee remarks in *The New American Literature*, "Nowhere can one find in English better models for study, better illustrations of all the devices of the modern and complicated art of short-story creation" (252).

Chapter Two

Prisoners of
Love and Marriage ⸺⸺⸺⸺⸺⸺

In *The Writing of Fiction*, Edith Wharton provides several definitions of the short story. One of them seems appropriate to the theme of individuals trapped by love and marriage. She tells us that the typical short story is "the foreshortening of a dramatic climax connecting two or more lives" (75). Each of the six stories examined in this chapter does indeed "foreshorten" a dramatic climax that not only connects, but frequently alters, and sometimes even transforms the lives of two or more of Wharton's protagonists. These heroes and heroines are either happy or disillusioned at the beginning of the narratives, but by the conclusion, they find themselves hopelessly entrapped in a situation that is, ironically, of their own making. Even those individuals who try to escape imprison themselves by accepting social censure or some other means of external control. Three of the tales, "The Lamp of Psyche," "The Line of Least Resistance," and "The Reckoning," are from Wharton's early period, and they are coupled with three, "The Letters," "Permanent Wave," and "The Day of the Funeral," from her major and late periods.[1] The later tales contain subject matter similar to that of the early stories and have been selected to demonstrate Wharton's thematic and technical development.

---

1. The material on "The Lamp of Psyche" and "The Letters" appeared in "Theme and Technique in the Tales of Edith Wharton" in the *Journal of the Short Story in English* 16 (Spring 1991): 41–49 and is reprinted with the permission of the editor.

In the early stories examined in this chapter, Wharton makes use of a variety of techniques to present her imprisonment theme. Most often, she selects an omniscient narrator to recount these short narratives, because this approach, Cynthia Griffin Wolff points out, "allowed her talent for irony full play" (156). Clearly irony pervades Wharton's early portrayals of her imprisoned protagonists. And frequently it is combined with blistering satire in her descriptions of the artificial upper-class society in which these entrapped individuals live.

Wharton also emphasizes symbolic settings in her early narratives. Descriptions of the natural landscape, interior decorations, and the statuary underscore the imprisonment of her central characters: Delia Corbett's terra cotta statue within enclosed ivied walls in "The Lamp of Psyche," Mindon's marble nymphs on a shrub-lined terrace in "The Line of Least Resistance," and Julia Westall's marble Greek slave between the folding doors of a back drawing room in "The Reckoning" reflect their entrapped lives. In particular, Wharton introduces the metaphor of the house with its different rooms to mirror the "condition in life" (Lewis 121) of her helpless victims of fate: Delia's aesthetically beautiful library, which epitomizes "the delicate ramifications of her husband's taste" (1: 46), Mindon's study, which is so heaped with his wife's bills that "it was bad for his digestion" (1: 218), and Julia's quietly subdued drawing room, which startles her with its "strangeness and unfamiliarity" (1: 423), all symbolize individuals imprisoned by love and marriage.

In her later tales, a significant development occurs in Wharton's short story artistry. She now emphasizes techniques that reveal the inner consciousness of her imprisoned protagonists—heart and hand imagery, the flashback, and the interior monologue. Lizzie West's pounding heartbeat in "The Letters," Nalda Craig's inward trembling in "Permanent Wave," and Ambrose Trenham's clammy, twitching hands in "The Day of the Funeral" provide the reader with an illuminating glance into the minds of these "trapped sensibilities." But even more revealing are Nalda's "excursions into the past" (Macauley and Lanning 155), which explain her dissatisfaction with her boring husband, Lizzie's frequent time shifts, which trace the idealization of her employer from their first meeting to the present, and Trenham's desperate inner deliberations, which expose the reasons for this self-indulgent man's adultery.

Finally, the late tales are replete with images of imprisonment: the locked doors and closing gates in "The Letters," the domestic jailer and steel clutch of the waver in "Permanent Wave," and the slipping bolts and clinking chains in "The Day of the Funeral" are striking reminders of the locked-in existence of Wharton's central characters.

"The Lamp of Psyche" (1895) is the first of Wharton's narratives to portray a wife's disillusionment and imprisonment in marriage. In this early uncollected tale, Wharton introduces many of the techniques that are characteristic of her early short fiction. Irony dominates the tale of Delia Corbett, who, after having been married only two months to a man she passionately worships, gradually becomes disillusioned by the discovery that her husband's actions are not worthy of "the most admirable man she had ever met" (1: 44). Symbolic settings in Paris and Boston reflect Delia's emotional state, and distinctive eye imagery mirrors the inner thoughts of Wharton's imprisoned central character. Satiric asides, beginning with Delia's acknowledgment that her upper-class lifestyle with Corbett is characterized by an "enjoyment of the purposeless" (1: 48), provide valuable insights into the modus vivendi of Parisian society at the turn of the century, and Wharton's penchant for classical allusion is evident from the title.

Delia Corbett, the "Psyche" of Wharton's story, is not the "beautiful damsel" (1: 42n) of the classical myth. Instead, the omniscient narrator informs us, she is "past thirty and had never been very pretty" (1: 42), a judgment with which Delia seemingly concurs as she looks in the mirror, "smiling carelessly at her insignificant reflection" (1: 43). Nonetheless, Delia is ecstatically happy as the narrative begins, because two months before, after a loveless first marriage (at nineteen she married a man with "beautiful blue eyes" and "a gardenia in his coat . . . these considerations had been the determining factors in her choice" [1: 44]) and two years of widowhood, she was given "the immense, the unapproachable privilege of becoming Laurence Corbett's wife" (1: 42). From the beginning of the tale, therefore, irony surfaces in Delia's dreamy musings on the extraordinary attributes of her second husband, a man "so obviously admirable that she wondered that people didn't stop her in the street to attest her good fortune" (1: 45). Moreover, Wharton sustains the irony throughout the narrative with her repeated use of the word "admirable" in her portrayal of this "most admirable" man's not-so-admirable behavior both in time of war and after.

The opening scene also introduces the reader to the magnificent ambience of the Corbetts' hotel suite, a setting reinforcing Wharton's dictum that character and setting are one (*WF* 84). The elegant Parisian drawing room and lush garden, "framed in ivied walls, with a mouldering terra-cotta statue in the center of its cup-shaped lawn" (1: 43), mirror Delia's entrapment as she reflects on her good fortune. Even the charming library, with its "expanse of harmonious bindings, the fruity bloom of Renaissance bronzes, and the imprisoned sunlight of two or three old pictures fitly epitomizing the delicate ramifications of her husband's taste" (1: 46) reflect her unhappy plight. In truth, Delia is both enchanted and imprisoned by the luxury surrounding her.

Wharton's irony intensifies as Corbett approaches his adoring wife at the beginning of the tale, and she once more marvels at his admirable appearance. She wonders if everyone judges him as "well-equipped" as she does, or if she walks "in a cloud of delusion, dense as the god-concealing mist of Homer" (1: 45). Looking into her husband's eyes, she sees only "the completeness of their communion" (1: 45). Eyes are of particular interest to Wharton (Russell, "Imagery" 457), and, as is the case here, she often refers to her characters' eyes as mirrors of their inner thoughts. Ironically, at the outset, Delia, like the Psyche of myth, is entrapped "in a cloud of delusion," and her eyes reflect her imprisoned state.

Corbett delivers a letter to his wife that brings news of her Bostonian Aunt Mary. The woman who provided "the chief formative influence of her niece's youth" (1: 48) has fallen, and after some discussion, the Corbetts decide to make the fateful trip to America to visit her. Cleverly, Wharton has made use of a letter to bring about a gradual awakening in her protagonist regarding her husband and their luxurious surroundings.

Wharton continues to emphasize interior decorations, paintings, and furnishings when the Corbetts arrive at her ailing Aunt Mary's house in Boston. Delia's reaction to its "discouraging hall, with a large-patterned oilcloth and buff walls stenciled with a Greek border," and its antiquated drawing room, with hard coal in the fireplace and "smoky expanses of canvas 'after' Raphael and Murillo which lurched heavily forward from the walls" (1: 49), once again reveals a consciousness entrapped by the superficialities characterizing her extravagant Parisian lifestyle. Although she hastily comments that her husband will not "like" her aunt's house, the reader soon realizes that it is she who no longer likes the "swell-fronted domicile" (1: 49) where she spent several years of her girlhood. Even more insight is provided into Delia's character when she assumes with embarrassment that the gown her aunt is wearing as she greets them "might have been an unaltered one of her mother's" (1: 49).

However, Wharton has introduced the unattractive Boston house and its altruistic resident to hasten the transformation in her protagonist. The narrator reveals that when Delia observes that her aunt, "a bundle of extraordinary vitalities" (1: 50), enjoys a "life of unadorned activity, the unsmiling pursuit of Purposes with a capital letter" (1: 48), she becomes increasingly aware that "her own life seem[s] vacuous, her husband's aims trivial as the subtleties of Chinese ivory carving" (1: 51). Wharton contrasts their lives to satirize—as she was wont to do—the "obvious inutility" (1: 48) of the lifestyle of the upper class. Corbett, an expatriate who has been a member of Parisian society for almost twenty-five years, is the object of an especially vitriolic attack when Wharton's protagonist awakens to the realization that her "so obviously admirable" husband really does nothing: "His elaborate intellectual processes bore no flower of result; he simply *was*" (1: 53).

Perhaps Delia might have dismissed her growing disenchantment with her husband had it not been for a conversation with her aunt regarding Corbett and his family background. Wharton fashions the abbreviated dialogue between the newlywed and her former guardian to intensify Delia's misgivings about her life and her husband's aims. When her Aunt Mary asks Corbett's age and pointedly inquires about his military service during the Civil War, her niece is forced to acknowledge, hesitantly, "I don't think he was in the war at all" (1: 52).

As she proffers this humiliating reply, Delia's face suddenly pales— Wharton often emphasizes facial coloration to reflect the inner conscious- ness of her protagonist—and her passionately patriotic aunt, widowed when her husband was killed at Bull Run, angrily retorts: "Why shouldn't he have been in the war?" (1: 52). This piercing question—a striking example of Wharton's assertion that "every phrase should be a sign-post" (*WF* 37)— soon occupies all of Delia's waking moments. Once imprisoned with unbridled admiration, she is now filled with silent condemnation. Not even a return to her beautiful surroundings in Paris is able to assuage her troubled state.

To provide the answer to the torturous question and end the emotional torment of her protagonist, Wharton interjects another brief but passionate conversation, this time between Delia and her husband. The "culminating moment" (*WF* 73) occurs when Corbett presents his wife with a pearl- studded framed miniature of an unknown United States cavalry officer inscribed with the date he was killed in battle. He bought the miniature for her so that it would be owned again by a fellow countryman, an ironic touch insofar as Delia has all but judged him a disloyal American.

Unable to restrain herself any longer, Delia takes his unwelcome gift and accusingly inquires, "Then why weren't you in the war?" (1: 56). Corbett, not wishing to meet her gaze as he had in the beginning of the narrative when "the completeness of their communion" linked them together, re- sponds, smiling: "I don't think I know . . . the truth is that I've completely forgotten the excellent reasons that I doubtless had at the time for remaining at home" (1: 56). With her face blazing with the passion she has stored for months, Delia blatantly labels him "a coward" (1: 57) and drops the miniature to the floor, shattering both its protective crystal and her dream of "the most admirable man she had ever met."

Until her Boston visit, the entrapped Delia's idealization of her husband, like the crystal protecting the face of the miniature, had shielded him from her closer scrutiny. When the crystal breaks, Delia's ideal is also destroyed. Like Henry James's smashed golden bowl, Wharton's shattered crystal provides a dramatic climax that symbolically destroys the illusions of her imprisoned heroine and restores her to reality. In marked contrast to the beginning of the story, when her unbounded happiness caused her to "burst out laughing" (1: 42), she now "burst[s] into tears" (1: 57).

In just an hour, however, Delia dries her tears and passes "a milestone in her existence" (1: 57). She realizes that her husband responded to her question with his customary "admirable air"; that she will no longer wallow "in a cloud of delusion"; and, most important, that although "her love had undergone a modification which the years were not to efface," she will inevitably "go on being in love with him" (1: 57).

Herein lies the one flaw in the execution of this early tale—the speed with which Delia's transformation occurs. At the opening of the narrative, and during the torturous period of indecision prior to questioning her husband about his military service, Wharton employs a soul-searching "excursion into the past" that provides a dramatic record of Delia's mental reactions "just as they come" (*WF* 12). Now, during the fateful hour that marked "a milestone in her existence," Wharton fails to enter into the consciousness of her protagonist. Instead, she mentions only that Delia acknowledges her "absurd" (1: 57) conduct and asks her husband's forgiveness.

The tale concludes as Delia has the shattered crystal replaced with "clear glass," an act symbolizing the substitution of "a tolerant affection" for "the passionate worship" (1: 57) she accorded her husband just a short time ago. Although she no longer idolizes her husband, she nonetheless chooses to remain entrapped in the same "imprisoned sunlight" that envelops the "two or three old pictures" in his luxurious library. Just as Psyche "took a lamp and looked at him [Cupid]" in the myth, so, too, Delia has looked more closely at her "admirable" lover, "bringing on herself considerable grief before they were reunited" (1: 42n).

Fifteen years later, during the major phase of her short story writing, Wharton wrote "The Letters" (1910), another tale of a woman's disillusionment and entrapment in marriage that contains remarkable similarities in subject matter and technique to "The Lamp of Psyche." At the beginning of the tale, Lizzie West, like Delia Corbett, is an ecstatically happy young woman in love with an "admirable" man; however, she, too, becomes disenchanted after her marriage to the "eminent and exceptional" (2: 180) Vincent Deering. Like the early tale, dramatic irony is evident in Lizzie's idealization of the "kind and tender" (2: 179) Deering, and Wharton's eye imagery once again highlights the imprisoned consciousness of her protagonist when she discovers that her husband had deceived her into marrying him.

In this later narrative, however, Wharton introduces a number of techniques that demonstrate an evolution in her artistry. Movements of the heart, masterful dialogue that "gather[s] up the loose strands of passion and emotion running through the tale" (*WF* 141), flashbacks, and interior monologues—techniques that reveal the innermost thoughts and feelings of Wharton's protagonist—reinforce the theme of imprisonment.

As the tale opens, the omniscient narrator paints Lizzie West, the young and pretty governess to Juliet Deering, daughter of Vincent Deering, a noted American artist, and his invalid wife, as "happy as a lark" (2: 181–82). Like Delia Corbett, she is in love, and her rapid heartbeat reflects her happy state. Throughout the narrative, Wharton exploits this innovative device—the movements of Lizzie's heart—to reveal her central character's emotional state: her heart beats faster when she feels secure in Deering's love; it drops and contracts when she becomes disillusioned and begins to question his motives.

In the first of several lengthy flashbacks—in contrast to "The Lamp of Psyche," where only one brief flashback at the beginning of the tale brings to light Delia's reflections on her first marriage—the reader learns that Lizzie has walked in a "vast golden haze" (2: 180) these past several months, a haze of love not unlike the "cloud of delusion" that entrapped the protagonist of the early tale. Wharton's initial shift to the past reveals the reason for Lizzie's enveloping haze. Six months before, tearfully upset that her pupil "would not work, would not obey" (2: 178), Lizzie met with her sympathetic employer, who assured her, with his "gentle" (2: 180) grey eyes, that she was good for Juliet and, more important, that she was good for him. Then he kissed her tears away. Lizzie dwells on the memory of that "first kiss" and the "sleeping germ of life" (2: 179) that it awakened in her.

This formerly "shy and sequestered" (2: 180) twenty-five-year-old also remembers the twice-weekly trysts with the more experienced Deering in museums and art galleries that followed her thrilling first kiss. She remembers, too, that "her heart beat so fast" (2: 181) whenever he discussed pictures and literature with her. Indeed, she soared to the heavens each time she heard him speak. Before long, intimate meetings in gardens and clandestine trips to the suburbs followed, and Lizzie, like Delia, became entrapped in her love and adoration for this man she deemed so perfect.

The narrator continues to move back and forth with brief flashes until a shift to the present reveals that Deering's wife has just died, and he must return to America to dispose of her property. Wharton's eye imagery, so prominent in "The Lamp of Psyche," also appears in this later narrative when Lizzie sees Deering prior to his departure. His tenderness and assurances of love leave her with "happy dizzy eyes" (2: 185). And just as Delia read in Corbett's eyes "the completeness of their communion" (1: 45), Lizzie sees a future with Deering in "the pact they sealed with their last look" (2: 185). She promises to write even though she fears comparisons with others more articulate than she. However, like Delia, who "knew herself to be capable of loving her husband better and pleasing him longer than any other woman in the world" (1: 42), Lizzie believes that her love for Deering—"no woman had ever loved him just as she had" (2: 186)—will compensate for her lack of expression. Alas, despite her frequent letters, the three missives Deering sends from the train and steamer make no mention of their future together.

R.W.B. Lewis maintains that Wharton invariably employs enclosed spaces—houses and rooms within houses—"to describe the inner nature of women" (121). In "The Letters," the narrator describes Lizzie's inner consciousness as "unfurnished" in the lonely years following Deering's departure. Although an inheritance has freed her from her impoverished state, her newly acquired fortune has not released her from her psychological prison. She remains, the narrator reveals, "like the possessor of an unfurnished house" (2: 191).

Not surprisingly, therefore, when Lizzie and Deering meet accidentally three years later, she soon realizes that although she is now engaged to the eligible Jackson Benn, Deering still remains "the one live spot in her consciousness" (2: 192). Her "dormant nerves" (2: 192) start to throb in his presence, and her heart begins "sounding in her ears the old confused rumor of the sea of life" (2: 194).

Nonetheless, despite these physical manifestations of deep feeling, Lizzie becomes increasingly provoked by Deering's evasive replies to her inquiries about his not having written a word, not even "a syllable" (2: 194), during his stay in America. She even asks if he ever read her letters (foreshadowing the end of the tale), and Deering, smiling, calculatingly counters, "There were beautiful, wonderful things in them" (2: 195).

Unlike "The Lamp of Pysche," wherein the conversations between Delia and Corbett signal only "culminating moments" (*WF* 73), in "The Letters," the lengthy exchanges between the heiress and her former employer following his deceptive reply link "speech to speech, one character catching up the phrase or point of the other's remark by way of challenge, question, matching of the idea and carrying it farther" (Beach 300). Lizzie becomes more emotional, more passionate, as she relentlessly questions Deering about his reasons for not writing, and he responds with a defense replete with explicit images of imprisonment: "Because I found, when I reached America, that I was a pauper; that my wife's money was gone, and that what I could earn—I've so little gift that way!—was barely enough to keep Juliet clothed and educated. It was as if an iron door had been locked and barred between us" (2: 195). In truth, it was Deering who locked this impressionable young girl out of his life, imprisoning her in her idealistic illusion of him. Nonetheless, Lizzie, her heart contracting, succumbs to his plea as compassionately as he had hoped, and the image of her fiancé disappears completely from view.

In the final section of the tale, the narrator jumps ahead another three years to the Deerings' son's second birthday. Once again, Wharton introduces the image of the house—the Deerings' "charming little house" (2: 197)—and its morning room—a room not unlike Corbett's beautiful Parisian library—to reflect the happy thoughts of her imprisoned victim before she becomes disillusioned with her husband.

As Lizzie and her friend, Andora Macy, busily unpack the trunks Deering left behind in a New York boardinghouse years before, the narrator once more enters the mind of Wharton's protagonist to reveal that she still remains entrapped in the "vast golden haze" that enveloped her at the beginning of the narrative:

> She only knew that each article she drew from the trunks sent through her the long tremor of Deering's touch. It was part of her wonderful new life that everything belonging to him contained an infinitesimal fraction of himself— a fraction becoming visible in the warmth of her love. (2: 199)

Imagine her devastation, therefore, when her old letters to Deering are discovered unopened in an embroidered bag found in one of the trunks. She knows at once that her husband lied when he told her that he had read "beautiful, wonderful things" in them. Obviously, her inheritance had played a significant role in his desire to make her his wife. Her heart drops sharply, and the golden haze that has surrounded her these last three years gives way to "some dark hollow" (2: 201) within. Like Delia Corbett, who was left to pick up the pieces of broken crystal when the illusion of her admirable husband is shattered, Lizzie is left to pick up her letters—"ten in all" (2: 201)—now that her vision of love has been similarly destroyed. As she looks around the disordered room, symbolic of the chaos and confusion she is presently experiencing, she compares her life to the "tarnished trash" (2: 201) scattered about her feet.

Wharton's imprisonment imagery is striking following the discovery of the unopened letters. Springing from her seat, Lizzie bolts the morning-room door and locks herself in the prison of her innermost thoughts. Peering out the window, she sees her husband leave the house and ponders, painfully, what her life would be like without him. Her heart contracts and then leaps once more—"she knew not whether up or down" (2: 205)—to signal her vacillating between leaving or remaining with her deceptive husband.

In contrast to "The Lamp of Psyche," where no insight is provided into the consciousness of Delia Corbett during that fateful hour following the shattering of her illusions about her admirable husband, in "The Letters," Wharton employs an extended interior monologue that takes the reader into the mind of her central character as she reflects on her three-year marriage and her feelings for the man who has deceived her:

> Those years were her whole life; everything before them had been colorless and unconscious, like the blind life of the plant before it reaches the surface of the soil. The years had not been exactly what she had dreamed; but if they had taken away certain illusions they had left richer realities in their stead. She understood now that she had gradually adjusted herself to the new image of her husband as he was, as he would always be. He was not the hero of her dreams, but he was the man she loved, and who had loved her. For she saw now, in this last wide flash of pity and initiation, that, as a comedy marble may be made out of worthless scraps of mortar, glass, and pebbles, so out of mean mixed substances may be fashioned a love that will bear the stress of life. (2: 206)

Consequently, at the tale's end, the reader understands why Lizzie still wants "only one thing—the life she had been living before she had given her baby the embroidered bag to play with" (2: 204).

Edith Wharton's story line and theme are very much the same in "The Lamp of Psyche" and "The Letters." She begins each story with a happy young woman in love with an "extraordinary" man, and she concludes with each protagonist disillusioned by the discovery that her husband's conduct has been neither admirable nor exceptional. Nonetheless, both women choose to remain imprisoned in their marriages, realizing that their love "had undergone a modification which the years were not to efface" (1: 57).

Similar techniques appear as well: irony, eye imagery, and the metaphor of the house as prison are prominent in both tales. However, there is a dramatic development in Wharton's deft use of time shifts from the early to the later tale. In "The Lamp of Psyche," she introduces only one flashback at the beginning of the story, but in "The Letters" she makes use of time shifts throughout. In fact, there are so many shifts from present to past and back to the present again in the first three sections of this seven-sectioned tale that at times the reader needs a respite. In the fifth section Wharton skips ahead two years, and in the final section there is another skip of three years. Significantly, these time shifts are not just "excursions into the past" to explain the present, but also glimpses into the future to enhance the reader's understanding of her central character. In effect, the continuous juxtaposition of past and present enables Wharton to explain the transformation that has occurred in Lizzie West. She is no longer an awestruck, naive, penniless servant. She and Deering have reversed roles: now he is dependent on her. (This development, too, marks a change from the early tale.) And, as before, Lizzie responds compassionately to his needs. Therefore, when the narrative concludes, it is clear why she decides to remain imprisoned with "the new image of her husband" (2: 206).

"The Line of Least Resistance" (1900), another uncollected tale from Wharton's early period, one that she considered "her finest story to date" (Lewis 125), is also a tale of disillusionment and entrapment in marriage. However, in this narrative it is not the wife, but rather the husband, Mindon, who becomes disillusioned, when he discovers that his self-centered, extravagant wife is having an affair with a family friend. Irony dominates his deliberations on his wife's infidelity and his declaration of freedom from her control. Satire and setting commingle in Wharton's description of the imprisoned Mindon, who is obsessed with providing costly accoutrements for his wife at his luxurious Newport villa even though "they yielded at best an indirect satisfaction" (1: 218). Wharton also experiments with a new technique: she makes striking use of time, carefully recording the hours slipping away, to dramatize Mindon's voluntary return to his marital prison "before it's too late" (1: 226).

Throughout the tale, Wharton restricts her narration to the consciousness of the imprisoned Mindon, and, as the story opens, she describes him quietly bemoaning the tardiness of his wife, Millicent, who, he complains, is "late—as usual" (1: 215). The word "late" and its ironic connotations are central to Wharton's portrayal of the wealthy Mindon, who has waited too long to free himself from the prison of his wife's control. The unforgettable key phrase, "late—as usual," therefore, contains Wharton's "germ of the whole" (*WF* 51), characterizing not only the behavior of Mindon's wife, but also, the reader soon discovers, the actions of Mindon himself.

Even Mindon's children do not escape his silent diatribe. When his two young daughters appear for lunch, he notes that they, too, are "unpunctual" (1: 215), a failing he attributes to their invariably unpunctual mother: "that accomplished woman had managed to transmit an acquired characteristic to her children" (1: 216). An exasperated mention of their tardiness provides the occasion for one child's remarking to her governess, "I don't mind vexing papa—nothing happens" (1: 217). This precocious response serves two purposes: it suggests that Mindon is also "late" in securing the respect of his children and, most important, it foreshadows the conclusion of the tale.

Mindon's ill-humor intensifies when he steps out on the luxurious terrace of his Newport villa. Guided by her belief that the descriptive passage "must depict only what the intelligence concerned would have noticed" (*WF* 85), Wharton is careful to point out those scenic details that symbolize the lifestyle her protagonist enjoys:

> The lawn looked as expensive as a velvet carpet woven in one piece; the flower borders contained only exotics; and the stretch of blue-satin Atlantic had the air of being furrowed only by the keels of pleasure boats. The scene, to Mr. Mindon's imagination, never lost the keen edge of its costliness. (1: 217)

The reader discovers, therefore, that Mindon considers his magnificent surroundings only in terms of their cost. However, neither the expensive marble nymphs on his shrub-lined terrace—they are not "worth the price"— nor his fine greenhouses—"he neither ate fruit nor wore orchids" (1: 218)—bring him happiness.

Mindon's discontent becomes even more obvious when he moves from room to room contemplating his luxurious lifestyle. His reflections in each room are, as Wharton intends, "event[s] in the history of [his] soul" (*WF* 85). In his study, he sees piles of bills that remind him, painfully, of his wife's extravagances; in the drawing room, he remembers banal conversations with listeners who "obviously resented his not being somebody else" (1: 218); in the dining room, he recalls long dinners with the dullest women he ever "languished between" (1: 219); in the ballroom, he visualizes the dancing that continued through the night even when he retired at eleven; and in the library, he glances at the abandoned books that no one in the house reads. In effect, Wharton's description of Mindon's odyssey through the rooms of his villa is replete with details that satirize upper-class society, enabling the reader to realize "not only the distinctions of class, but the motivations that underlie the characters' being and doing" (Kimbel 48).

Next Mindon proceeds to his wife's boudoir, "the center of Millicent's complex social system" (1: 219), and his eyes are immediately drawn to her writing table. In contrast to his, which overflows with bills, hers is filled with invitations, notes, cards, and correspondence—a jumbled assortment symbolizing her inability to "live without novelty" (1: 217). Indeed, Mindon has placed his entire income "practically at Millicent's disposal" (1: 218), and he feels entrapped by his wife's extravagant self-indulgence. And his entrapment is exacerbated by the discovery of a letter (as in "The Lamp of Psyche," a letter plays a significant role in this early story) that reveals that Millicent is having an affair with a family friend.

Suddenly, the walls of the boudoir—the wall is a familiar image of imprisonment in Wharton's tales—pose the question, "And who are you?" (1: 219). No longer willing to wallow in "bewildered subjection" (1: 220), he angrily retorts: "I'll tell you, by God. I'm the man that paid for you" (1: 219–20). Strutting across the room, he proceeds to declare his independence: "Why, of course, the room belonged to him, the house belonged to him, and he belonged to himself! . . . For years he had been the man that Millicent thought him, the mere projection of her disdain; and now he was himself" (1: 220). He mistakenly believes that by openly repudiating his wife as his jailer, he will recover his identity and liberate himself from continued imprisonment.

The striking of the clock—the first of Wharton's dramatic mentions of time in this early narrative—also serves as a reminder to Mindon of his "unpunctuality" in freeing himself from his wife's control. It jolts him into a false "sense of lucidity" (1: 220), which Wharton describes with language as complex and confusing as the perplexing messages penetrating the consciousness of her distraught protagonist:

> His brain was like a brightly-lit factory, full of flying wheels and shuttles. All the machinery worked with the greatest rapidity and precision. He was planning, reasoning, arguing, with unimagined facility; words flew out like sparks from each revolving thought. But suddenly he felt himself caught in the wheels of his terrific logic, and swept round, red and shrieking, till he was flung off into space. (1: 220)

Wharton does not report what "his terrific logic" revealed. The reader is informed only that suddenly, without explanation, Mindon decides to leave his home for a cheap hotel nearby. Just as in "The Lamp of Psyche," where the reader is given no insight into the consciousness of Delia Corbett prior to her hasty decision to ask her husband's forgiveness, here the reader is not made aware of what thoughts pass through Mindon's mind prior to his abrupt departure from home.

The slumlike hotel room to which he escapes is yet another striking example of Wharton's use of an enclosed space to mirror the depressing thoughts of her imprisoned central character. The squalid furnishings—the smell of cheap soap, the "shower of dead flies" from the jarred window, the "burnt matches and a fuzz of hair" in the dressing table drawer (1: 221)— provide a striking contrast to the splendid accoutrements of the mansion he has forsaken. Moreover, the pictures of the "Landing of Columbus" and General Grant that adorn the shabby walls are tragically ironic insofar as both men were heroes, while Mindon is a defeated man.

Dramatic references to time reappear as he begins to wonder whether his wife is at all disturbed by his unexplained absence. The clock struck in Millicent's boudoir when Mindon first declared his independence; his watch now records his ever-increasing waves of doubt; and by the time he checks the time again, he will have decided to bend to the pressures of home and family and return to his imprisoned state.

In the final section of the tale, therefore, Mindon summons his physician, his uncle and senior partner, and his rector, whose first remark, "Thank heaven, we are not too late!" (1: 223), is markedly ironic in that he has called these men together only to acquire an excuse to return home. After he delivers a tirade on Millicent's wrongdoings—not unlike the monologue introduced at the beginning of the tale, when he was without a captive audience—the emissaries urge him to return home "before it's too late" (1: 226).

They do not realize that although it may not be too late for Mindon to return to his wife, it is already too late for him to free himself from his imprisoned state. "It's for the children" (1: 226), he hypocritically stammers to the departing trio as he follows them back to his wife's control, ironically confirming his daughter's earlier prediction that even when papa is vexed, "nothing happens." Despite his protestations to the contrary, Wharton's imprisoned central character realizes that he does not belong to himself: he belongs to Millicent and to the moneyed prison to which he has voluntarily decided to return.

"Permanent Wave" (1935), a thematic companion tale to "The Line of Least Resistance," was written about thirty-six years later and is one of Wharton's final tales. Nalda Craig, an imperfect wife remarkably similar to Mindon's Millicent, is also self-indulgent, prone to extravagance, and engaged in an affair with a charming man. In fact, she intends to elope with her exciting explorer, until she discovers, like Mindon, that it is "too late" for her to escape her married prison.

As in "The Line of Least Resistance," dramatic irony sustains the tale. Ironically, an egocentric wife has deluded herself into believing she can flee from her monotonous but otherwise comfortable marriage without remorse. Likewise, references to time appear repeatedly in this late tale, in particular, in Wharton's detailed description of the hours Nalda spends having her hair permed "in the steel clutch of the waver" (2: 793).

However, in contrast to the early tale, Wharton employs mocking satire that pervades the entire narrative. She is especially humorous when she describes her protagonist's ruminations on her social position, her looks, and her clothing. Finally, Wharton introduces a mistaken date, an artistic device that occasions the surprise ending for the tale—Nalda's decision to remain imprisoned "everyday for the rest of her life" (2: 797) with her "domestic jailer" (2: 799).

The tale begins as Nalda Craig hurries to her hairdresser's with her husband's derisive epithet, "late as usual" (2: 789), echoing in her brain. Immediately, the reader is struck by the reappearance of this phrase from Wharton's earlier "The Line of Least Resistance," where another husband makes this same disparaging remark about his habitually tardy spouse. Nalda, like Mindon's Millicent, is always accused of being late by her husband, and she acknowledges, unhappily, that she is "always a little late to [her] engagements" (2: 791). However, she objects to her husband always delivering the jibe in "that irritating level voice of his" (2: 789), an observation that suggests that she, like Mindon, may be entrapped in a less-than-perfect marriage. She knows she is late for her appointment for a permanent wave—a whole day behind, her disgruntled hairdresser informs her. Nonetheless, she successfully cajoles him into letting her slip in ahead of those waiting.

In the first of several extended interior monologues in this late narrative, Wharton's central character discloses the reasons for her discontent with her hypercritical husband. The reader learns that years before, Nalda had pursued Vincent Craig, renowned lecturer in economics at the University, when she realized how well-known he was in his profession and how much she would be noticed just by becoming his wife. However, she soon discovered, much to her dismay, that her husband was always buried in his books or preoccupied with his academic and literary obligations and was not "at every moment acutely conscious of her looks, her clothes, her graces, of what she was thinking or feeling" (2: 790).

As Nalda's monologue continues, the reader also learns that six months before, she met Phil Ingerson, an "endlessly exciting" (2: 791) explorer, who, unlike her husband, appreciatively scrutinizes everything about her and even "measure[s] his hours by her comings and goings" (2: 792). Although Nalda recognizes Phil's predilection for pretty women—he originally came to Kingsbridge because he was tracking down an attractive girl he met on a West Indian cruise—and his preoccupation with exploration, she is still very much attracted to the lifestyle of this would-be archaeologist.

In fact, she has decided to elope with him—but not without the perm that caused him to notice her at their first meeting. In the short time she has known him she has had four perms, and "he never failed to notice when she had been newly waved!" (2: 791).

Images of imprisonment abound as Nalda sits "in the steel clutch of the waver" dreamily reflecting on the past. She likens the time it takes to get her hair permed to "serving a life sentence" (2: 791). Nonetheless, she endures the "four hours' immobility," pondering Phil's smiles and laughter and his "odd paradoxical judgments of life and men" (2: 791), because she is certain the end result—the perm—will fulfill her dream of happiness with "the man who was to remake her life . . . " (2: 791; Wharton's ellipsis).

Wharton also provides the reader with illuminating insights into the shallow mentality and purposeless concerns of the society matrons sitting around Nalda who are also waiting for their time in the steel waver to be over: she mocks their lifestyle with her masterful mimicking of their pretentious dialogue. One woman moans over problems with her new help—"I never choose a day for this but just as I start there's a rumpus at home"—while another complains about her cook—"What I always say is, it pays in the end to get your groceries sent from New York"—and a third comments about the fashion scene—"I see they're going to wear those uncrushable velvets a good deal this winter" (2: 794).

Nalda tries to block out this idle chatter during her "four hours' imprisonment" (2: 791). However, her desire for a dress of this new uncrushable velvet, her concern that Phil may be "as fussy as other men about too much luggage" (2: 794), and her fear that she will not be able to find a good hairdresser in Central America suggests a growing apprehension about her impending elopement. She fears she may be replacing her present imprisonment with another that will be even more intolerable. Especially telling is her wish that the waving be over so that she will have no more time to think about this eventuality: the four hours entrapped in the waver are too long to be imprisoned in her own consciousness.

As in "The Line of Least Resistance," Wharton dramatically uses time to dramatize her protagonist's return to her unexciting spouse. When Nalda leaves the salon, satisfied and self-confident, she informs her hairdresser that his calendar is a day ahead, and he retorts (in error): "it's you who are behind the times, Mrs. Craig. I always pull off the leaf [of the calendar] first thing every morning, myself" (2: 795).

Nalda mistakenly believes, therefore, that she has missed the day of her elopement. In a mild state of shock, she wanders the streets imagining another of her husband's reproaches sounding in her troubled consciousness: "Nalda never knows the day of the week. She says it would only cramp her style if she did . . . " (2: 796; Wharton's ellipsis). Her recently acquired self-confidence vanishes as she concludes that Phil must have left that morning without her:

> The expedition came first in his mind—that fact had always been clear to Nalda. . . . And if a poor little woman, who had imagined she couldn't live without him, got cold feet at the last minute, and failed to turn up—well, with the exploring fever on him, he'd probably take even that with a shrug, for he was committed to the enterprise, and would have to go without her if she failed him. (2: 796–97)

With these distressing thoughts gnawing at her brain, Nalda finally reaches home. She drags herself up the stairs to her room and notices the tear in the stair carpet that her husband has been constantly nagging her to have repaired. As she surveys the tear—which can be symbolically compared to the "great holes" (2: 797) in her mind these past few months—she realizes, suddenly, that she has been so distracted by her attentive, unpredictable explorer that she has not given careful thought to the consequences of leaving her comfortable, though inattentive, husband.

Not surprisingly, therefore, when Nalda discovers that she, not the hairdresser, was correct about the day of the week and that she still has time to elope with Phil, she decides that it is "too late" to escape her "domestic jailer." The hours of immobility that began with thoughts of the "endlessly exciting" Phil concluded with the realization that she is more interested in uncrushable velvet than the Yucatan ruins, that her departure would cause her husband much pain and suffering, and that "the reality of that other future" (2: 797) is, like the perm, only an illusion.

The tale ends as Nalda laughs hysterically and loses consciousness while murmuring "poor old Vincent" (2: 800), the phrase she repeats whenever she is overcome with feelings of guilt. In this concluding scene, Wharton effects a striking irony when Nalda's husband, hovering over his wife's prostrate body, pushes back "her suffocating hair, composing her limbs as if, with pious hands, he were preparing her for her final rest. . . . " (2: 800; Wharton's ellipsis). This comforting gesture parallels his wife's casting aside her illusions of a life with an "exciting explorer" in preparation for "serving a life sentence" (2: 791) with him.

Both "The Line of Least Resistance" and "Permanent Wave" portray protagonists who feel entrapped in their marriages; both feel undervalued. Hence, Mindon suddenly runs off by himself, and Nalda impulsively decides to elope with another man. Both discover, however, that it's too late to escape their imprisoned lives—they are inextricably bound to their less-than-perfect spouses.

Wharton also makes use of many of the same techniques in these tales. Attention-getting openers, dramatic irony, and comic satire expose the societal pressures that compel her protagonists to remain in their married prisons. But there are also techniques in the later tale that do not appear in "The Line of Least Resistance," namely, the flashback device and a surprise ending. In "Permanent Wave," Wharton makes extensive use of the flashback to explain Nalda's initial attraction and subsequent marriage to Vincent Craig. Shifts to the past also acquaint the reader with Phil, the other man in Nalda's life, and the reasons for her fascination with him. (In the early tale, Millicent does not appear, and little is revealed about her lover—only that he brings gifts to the children.) These flashbacks, therefore, enhance the reader's understanding of Wharton's protagonist.

Just as important is the surprise ending of the late tale. "Mrs. Wharton was fond of trick endings," Granville Hicks points out, "and was not above relying on coincidences and other contrivances" (17). Vincent Craig's surprising disclosure that Nalda is, in fact, correct about the day of the week does give her time to revert to her original plan to elope. However, she does not consider that possibility. Instead, she sentences herself to continue her "monotonous married years" (2: 797), allowing Wharton a more impressive ending than that of the early tale, where Mindon's return is not unexpected.

"The Reckoning" (1902) introduces the final set of tales of disillusionment and entrapment in marriage to be examined in this chapter. Unlike the tales already discussed, where the imprisoned victims opt to remain with their marital jailers, in "The Reckoning," Wharton recounts the story of Julia Westall, a wife who is not given the choice: she is summarily rejected by her second spouse. Years before, Julia callously left her egocentric first husband to free herself from the bondage of a conventional marriage. Ironically, she is crushed when her present husband requests his freedom for the same reason. The narrative is distinguished for its dramatic opening, animated dialogue, and memorable epigrams. Wharton's mocking satire also emerges in this early tale, particularly in the opening paragraphs, in her cynical description of the pretentious Van Sideren social circle: they welcome the Westalls' unorthodox view of marriage because they believe that "all the audacities [are] artistic" (1: 421). And, once again, irony sustains Wharton's portrayal of a woman who is devastated by her own unconventional "religion of personal independence" (1: 424).

Wharton launches "The Reckoning" with one of her most provocative beginnings: "The marriage law of the new dispensation will be: *Thou shalt not be unfaithful—to thyself*" (1: 420). This dramatic opener condemning unfaithfulness to oneself bears out her conviction that if the narrator's "first stroke be vivid and telling the reader's attention will be instantly won" (*WF* 51–52). Moreover, the declaration encapsulates the theme of the entire narrative. Clement Westall, an attorney of some note, expounds this unconventional marriage law during his Saturday talk at the exclusive Van Sideren studio. The artificial Van Siderens, Wharton reveals satirically, have been accepted in upper-class society only because they have a studio where they serve whiskey and soda and exhibit paintings of "purple grass and a green sky" (1: 421). They are fascinated by the unconventional in art and behavior—hence their interest in Westall's unorthodox "marriage law of the new dispensation."

Westall's wife, Julia, however, is disturbed by her husband's lecture. Although she had originally championed "the law of fidelity to one's self" and is, in fact, responsible for proselytizing him, she now has misgivings about "the articles of her faith" (1: 421). Wharton's revealing eye imagery exposes the reason for Julia's disquiet—Una Van Sideren, the pretty twenty-six-year-old daughter of the Herbert Van Siderens. With her "large limpid eyes" (1: 421), she seems hypnotized by Westall's presentation. Julia's resentment builds as she sees her husband smiling appreciatively at Una's mesmerized glances. From the beginning of the tale, therefore, the reader is aware that Julia is imprisoned by feelings of inadequacy that surface with her husband's public espousal of "the immorality of marriage" (1: 421).

That evening, still troubled by her husband's talk, Julia nervously requests that he no longer discuss "such things" (1: 423) in public. She looks around the drawing room and becomes lost in the somber images that have witnessed so many of their intimate conversations. The "shaded lamps, the quiet-colored walls hung with mezzotints, the pale spring flowers scattered here and there" (1: 423)—a symbolic setting that "establish[es] tone" and "provide[s] insight into the characters" (McDowell, *Wharton* 82)—parallel her own despondent spirit. She is reminded, painfully, of another drawing room, a room she shared with her first husband, which was distinguished by its picture of a Roman peasant and statue of a Greek slave, symbols of the bondage she wished to escape.

Julia is reluctant to let Westall know why she prefers that he not lecture on the new law of marital freedom. She does not wish to tell him that she has returned to a more traditional view of the marriage bond, that she no longer espouses an unorthodox approach to marriage. She intuits that her husband has a "special reason" (1: 423) for promulgating the principles on which their marriage was based, and she fears hearing what that reason might be.

Consequently, when he argues that "the law of fidelity to one's self" should be publicly proclaimed and asks why she wishes him to stop his series of talks, Julia responds only that such discussions should not be within earshot of a young girl like Una Van Sideren. Still suffering from feelings of inferiority and jealousy, she offers reasons why Una's presence should not be allowed. At one point she even asks her husband if he would like to marry someone like Una, and, to her surprise, he replies that he would, "if she were my kind of girl in other respects" (1: 425). He then ends the conversation with a further admission about the object of Julia's distress: "She interests me" (1: 425).

These comments evoke painful memories of the past for Julia. Wharton introduces her only flashback—a technique that she employs infrequently in her early narratives—to reveal her protagonist's recollections of her failed first marriage. Powerful images of imprisonment parallel the feelings of entrapment Julia experienced during those unhappy years married to John Arment, an arbitrary, selfish man whose personal needs were all that mattered to him. She remembers feeling that

> her husband's personality seemed to be closing gradually in on her, obscuring the sky and cutting off the air, till she felt herself shut up among the decaying bodies of her starved hopes. A sense of having been decoyed by some world-old conspiracy into this bondage of body and soul filled her with despair. If marriage was the slow lifelong acquittal of a debt contracted in ignorance, then marriage was a crime against human nature. She, for one, would have no share in maintaining the pretense of which she had been a victim: the pretense that a man and a woman, forced into the narrowest of personal relations, must remain there till the end. (1: 427)

Although at the time Julia thought that "in a blind rudimentary way" Arment might possess some potential for feeling and suffering, she chose not to prolong her marital imprisonment to endure "the laborious process of [his] growing up" (1: 426). She left, feeling certain that he never understood the reasons why she no longer wanted him.

She felt bruised and wounded following the divorce from Arment. Dramatic epigrams on individual freedom versus the bondage of conventional relationships appear as Julia remembers the aftermath of her miserable first marriage and the unorthodox ideas she advocated at that time. Her belief that "no marriage need be an imprisonment" gradually led her to conclude that "people grew at varying rates, and the yoke that was an easy fit for the one might soon become galling to the other. That was what divorce was for: the readjustment of personal relations" (1: 427).

Now, after ten years of marriage to Westall, Julia no longer adheres to her gospel of change and renewal. She does not wish the new law to apply to their union. She has reverted to the standards of a traditional marriage whereby "he and she were one" (1: 428). However, she fears that her husband does not share her newfound conviction.

Subsequently, Julia once again engages Westall in a painful conversation regarding his Saturday talks. Her words are laced with stumbling and stammering, a technique Wharton frequently employs to signal the extent of her protagonist's distress: "I can't bear to have you speak as if—as if—our marriage—were like the other kind—the wrong kind" (1: 429). She finally admits she no longer recognizes the universality of her unconventional marital code. In response, her husband callously invokes the doctrine of individual liberty and reveals his intention to leave her to marry someone else, the young and impressionable Una Van Sideren.

Wharton narrates the final section of the tale solely from the consciousness of Julia, allowing the reader an intimate look at her inconsolable protagonist as she painfully attempts to maintain her grasp on reality. Like Mindon in "The Line of Least Resistance," she summons her possessions in an attempt to bolster her fading self-esteem. In words not unlike Mindon's, she cries out, "This is my room—this is my house" (1: 431). Her declarations, however, have a hollow sound, for she cannot repair her damaged ego in a house with rooms "with which she had never been able to establish any closer relation than that between a traveler and a railway station" (1: 423). In truth, she still belongs to the man who has rejected her.

Moreover, she knows that she alone is responsible for what has happened to her. The rationale she invoked to escape the imprisonment of her oppressive first marriage—"the law of fidelity to one's self"—is the cause of her present state. Ironically, she has imprisoned herself: "She was the prisoner of her own choice: she had been her own legislator, and she was the predestined victim of the code she had devised" (1: 431–32).

Her contemplation of her plight ends when, suddenly, like Mindon, she leaves the house. Once again, Wharton does not enter the consciousness of her protagonist to provide an explanation for her hasty departure. She does, however, introduce a number of depressing images to emphasize her protagonist's devastating sense of loss: "With an aimless haste," Julia roams "the long empty street," watching "meaningless faces" (1: 432) drifting by. The "bare and hideous" streets; the "shabby houses, with rows of ash barrels behind bent area railings" (1: 432); the "low-ceilinged" empty restaurant with its "grayish lumpy salt," "discolored metal teapot," "black and bitter" tea; and the "fissured pavement" (1: 433) also mirror her desolate, alienated state.

On an impulse, she stops at the home of her first husband. Although he is shocked by the appearance of his unexpected visitor, Arment leads his former wife to the familiar drawing room, where she recognizes the contadina on the chimney and the statue of the Greek slave—images of imprisonment that characterized her first marriage. Once again, sentence breaks and hesitations underscore Julia's admission that her husband has left her. Dramatically ironic is her humiliating confession that just as Arment did not understand why she tired of him, she does not understand why Westall has tired of her. After acknowledging the destructive nature of her "religion of personal independence," she even admits that when she left him ten years before, she did not consider his "potentialities of feeling, of suffering" (1: 426), nor did she care that he did not understand why she left him. She asks for his forgiveness, "for not understanding that *you* didn't understand. . . . " (1: 437; Wharton's ellipsis).

The tale concludes as Arment's footman, "evidently alive to his obligations" (1: 437), comes forward to let her out into the darkness. But Wharton does not intend that these final lines signal only the footman's awareness of the responsibilities of his position. They also provide a final ironic thrust at Julia's past failure to recognize "the obligation that love creates" (1: 436). She is left alone in the darkness, the imprisoned victim of the "inner law" she once renounced, "the prisoner of her own choice" (1: 431).

"The Day of the Funeral" (1933), written almost twenty years later, also deals with the painful aftermath of rejection, only in this late tale, the husband's infidelity leads to his twofold repudiation. Ambrose Trenham, a professor at Kingsborough University, attempts to rationalize his adulterous conduct (conduct that provoked his wife's suicide) when his mistress departs, leaving him, like Julia Westall, with "a dreadful sense of loneliness" (2: 686). A startling beginning and an impressive setting with "dark deserted streets" (2: 685), not unlike those found in "The Reckoning," distinguish this late tale; and, as with its early counterpart, irony dominates Wharton's portrayal of a man "who could not live without tenderness, without demonstrative tenderness" (2: 675).

In "The Reckoning," the reader is not made aware of the reasons for Julia's visit to her first husband or her acknowledgment of guilt for having left him years before. In this later narrative, however, Wharton provides a number of interior monologues that reveal the motives for the behavior of this self-centered man who "follow[s] his instinct" (2: 676) and never accepts responsibility for his actions. She also makes lavish use of dialogue in this late tale. And she plays with words, in particular, with a profusion of negatives to spotlight "the dreary void" (2: 685) resulting from the life lost.

Lewis, in his biography of Wharton, terms the first lines of "The Day of the Funeral" "Edith Wharton's briskest opening gambit" (523): "His wife had said: 'If you don't give her up I'll throw myself from the roof.' He had not given her up, and his wife had thrown herself from the roof" (2: 669). However, Wharton does not present this shocking beginning just to startle the reader. She makes it clear in *The Writing of Fiction* that

> the arrest of attention by a vivid opening should be something more than a trick. It should mean that the narrator has so brooded on this subject that it has become his indeed, so made over and synthesized within him that, as a great draughtsman gives the essentials of a face or landscape in a half-a-dozen strokes, the narrator can "situate" his tale in an opening passage which shall be a clue to all the detail eliminated. (52–53)

Hence, she situates her tale with this dramatic opener and slips easily into Trenham's reflections on his wife's threat and the happenings since her suicide. His interior monologue is replete with a succession of negatives to reaffirm Mrs. Trenham's loss of life: "Nothing" of her warning to him was revealed; she left "no letters or diary—no papers of any sort"; she "never" owned much; and she was "never 'quite right' " (2: 669) after the death of her only child. Negatives continue as Wharton exposes Ambrose Trenham's dispassionate response to his wife's suicide. He could "never" recall the aftermath: he had "no" family, his house seemed "never" his, and when he was asked what he wanted engraved on her coffin, he responded, "Nothing" (2: 669). Clearly, there is no expression of regret or sadness from this man who has just lost his wife.

Wharton also employs negatives in the description of her protagonist at his wife's funeral. Although he is usually "unobservant," usually "not conscious" of intentionally seeking out faces, he possesses the "uncanny faculty for singling out everyone whom he knew in the crowded church. It was incredible" (2: 670). Exiting the church, he suddenly sees his mistress, Barbara Wake, and terms her "indecent" (2: 670) for coming to the funeral. Ironically, he views her as the cause of the tragedy—"The woman tempted me"—and vows "never" (2: 670) to see her again. Obviously attempting to free himself from any feelings of guilt, Trenham blames someone else for the tragedy that has occurred.

Consequently, during "the endless day, the empty hours after the funeral" (2: 670), he decides that he must punish Barbara for his wife's death and his distress. He will gather her letters and photograph so that he can send them back "without a word" (2: 671). Then he will dismiss his former lover without comment.

Negatives reappear when Trenham suddenly feels hungry and embarrassedly asks the housemaid for lunch. Hoping that she does not think him "unfeeling, unheroic" (2: 671), he eats ravenously when the food is placed before him. He even seems to experience a kind of "resurrection" (2: 672) after filling his stomach with food. Ironically, he believes that by satisfying his hunger, he can also assuage what little guilt he feels. Unfortunately, the relief he experiences after eating is short-lived. Thoughts of his wife distress him—"If she could only know how he was suffering and atoning already" (2: 673)—but, as before, his reflections center on his own distress. After all, his wife's suicide has effected the ultimate horror—his being left alone.

At this point in the narrative, Wharton makes liberal use of her central character's hands to reflect his innermost thoughts and feelings. She portrays Trenham's hands as "clammy" (2: 673) when he writes a note to Barbara. She notes that his fingers begin to twitch when he ties the large envelope holding the letters. And she describes his hand as "shaking" (2: 673) when he addresses the packet. Of course, the need to devise an appropriate strategy to return the dozens of unwanted letters adds to his emotional distress.

Wharton creates the perfect setting to highlight Trenham's painful trek to his lover's house. As he treads the "deserted" streets of the Kingsborough suburbs, the "cold and moonless" night and the "scantily lit" street (2: 674) mirror his gloomy state. Like the bare streets and "fissured pavement" (1: 433) that characterize Julia's cracked and abandoned spirit in "The Reckoning," "the hanging boughs of old elms" (2: 674), a striking image of enclosure, suggest, symbolically, Wharton's middle-aged protagonist.

Heading toward the garage, their "desolate trysting place" (2: 674), he is haunted by thoughts of his dead wife. He finds it inconceivable that she had taken her own life. She had been so reserved that he, a man with "irresistible" (2: 675) needs, had not dreamed that she was so much like him. He realizes that there was passion in his shy and reticent wife had he taken the time to discover it: "Now he understood that her cold reluctant surrender concealed a passion so violent that it humiliated her, and so incomprehensible that she had never mastered its language" (2: 675). He rationalizes that had he known of his wife's "springs of passion" (2: 675), he would not have sought another woman. Like Julia Westall, he ignored the "inner law" in marriage—to love as well as to be loved. He even acknowledges that it was he who seduced and corrupted Barbara and ironically concludes that instead of dismissing her from his life, "he owed her something!" (2: 677).

However, when he meets her in the garage and she informs him that she is leaving the next day for California, his response seems to suggest that she owes him something: "You can't go—you can't leave me like this! . . . Are you afraid of what people might say? Is that it? How can they say anything when they know we're going to be married? Don't you know we're going to be married? . . . What are you afraid of?" (2: 678–79). Ironically, he is afraid that if she finds someone younger, richer, more glamorous than he, she will reject his magnanimous offer of marriage. He is afraid, too, that if she leaves him, there will be no one to fill the void that his wife has left. He will be all alone, and "he couldn't face that sense of being alone again" (2: 682).

But when she assures him there is no one else she wishes to marry, he becomes suddenly euphoric—he has found a replacement for his wife. In fact, he is so exhilarated that he embraces her passionately and accidentally scatters her letters all over the floor. Once more, Wharton relies on the discovery of a letter to sustain the imprisonment of her protagonist. Quickly Barbara's eyes scan the note that he had written to her earlier that day: "You will probably feel, as I do, that after what has happened you and I can never—" (2: 680).

Immediately Trenham injudiciously explains that he wrote the note when he wanted her to share the burden of responsibility for his wife's death: "I couldn't bear the horror alone. Like a miserable coward I let myself think you were partly responsible" (2: 681). He even tells her of his wife's frequent warnings that she would kill herself if he continued his adulterous conduct.

These shocking revelations horrify Barbara, and for several moments she is unable to speak. Jean Frantz Blackall points out that intervals of silence, in addition to sentence breaks and pauses, are commonplace in Wharton's narratives, when she "represent[s] the inexpressible, or that which a character is unwilling to express." When Barbara finally regains her composure, she whispers repeatedly, "I never dreamed she knew" (2: 682). Again a period of silence ensues until her self-indulgent lover acknowledges his guilt and pleads for pity. But Barbara, experiencing her own guilt, feels no pity for him. In a lengthy outburst laden with ellipses, she passionately cries out, "The only pity I feel is for *her*" (2: 683). She even accuses Trenham of impatiently waiting for his wife to kill herself: "And now you come here, when the earth's hardly covered her, and try to kiss me, and ask me to marry you—and think, I suppose, that by doing so you're covering up her memory more securely, you're pounding down the earth on her a little harder. . . . " (2: 684; Wharton's ellipsis). Finally, she reaffirms her intention to go away. She fears that if she remains, she might eventually forgive him.

A desolate Trenham returns home along the same "dark deserted streets" (2: 685) he traveled a short time ago. His life, like the streets, is also dark and deserted. The negatives so prominent at the beginning of the tale recur as he ponders Barbara's rejection. He rationalizes that he went to see her with the intention of ending their relationship, and she simply agreed with him: "But after all nothing is changed—absolutely nothing. I went there to tell her that we should probably never want to see each other again; and she agreed with me. She agreed with me—that's all" (2: 685). He is still unable to acknowledge any wrongdoing. Just as he denies any responsibility for his wife's death, so, too, he evades responsibility for driving his mistress away. Nonetheless, he feels rejected, deserted.

Wharton returns to the image of the house to mirror her downcast protagonist. As he looks within himself to salvage his damaged ego, the inside of his head seems like a deserted house: "It was empty, absolutely empty" (2: 685). However, he is relieved by the appearance of a "small speck of consciousness [that] appeared in the dreary void" (2: 685). He conjectures that it may be a replacement for his departed lover. He even smiles and feels "a faint warmth" at the thought that "nothing is changed— absolutely nothing."

Wharton's images of imprisonment surface prominently when he finally reaches his doorstep and discovers that he has no key, that he is "locked out of his own house" (2: 685). Exasperated by what he perceives as a further rejection, he wants to cry. But before tears appear, he is rescued by his solicitous maid. As the tale concludes, Professor Ambrose Trenham hears "that familiar slipping of the bolts and clink of the chain" locking him into his house, where he is left with a "dreadful sense of loneliness" (2: 686).

"The Reckoning" and "The Day of the Funeral" contain certain striking resemblances. Both of Wharton's protagonists ignored the "inner law" in marriage—to love as well as to be loved. Although Julia Westall admits that her first husband may have had the potential to change his egotistical behavior, she did not choose to wait: she left him without an explanation. Trenham also did not take the time to discover the passion in his wife: he simply found it in another. The ultimate irony in both tales is that in gaining their individual freedoms, Wharton's protagonists have lost the person they wanted most and are left alone, each imprisoned in "his own house" (2: 686).

Dramatic openings, symbolic settings, and hand and eye imagery high-light both narratives. However, there is a marked development in Wharton's use of dialogue in the later tale. In "The Reckoning," the stops and repeti-tions between husband and wife as they discuss their positions on the new marriage code affect the reader as they do Julia—"with a sudden rush of weariness" (1: 422). Moreover, Julia's faltering speech—and her need for a nerve tonic—seem to contradict Wharton's portrayal of her protagonist as a spirited, assertive woman who, despite her "reversion" (1: 428) to the old marriage law, should have little difficulty asserting her changed beliefs. Even her emotionless reply to her husband's painful disclosure that he intends to leave her to marry someone else—"I wish you good luck" (1: 430)—lacks credibility. In contrast, in "The Day of the Funeral," Wharton creates an emotion-filled conversation between Barbara and Trenham that abounds with "half-utterances, challenges, questions, meanings developed through the give-and-take of dialogue" (Beach 299). Filling half the tale, their heated emotional exchanges bespeak his unremitting self-centeredness and her hypocritical remorse. Although the dialogue at times appears somewhat melodramatic, it serves not only "to emphasize the crises of the tale," as Wharton intends, "but to give it as a whole a greater effect of continuous development" (*WF* 73). Clearly, Barbara's passionate outbursts convince Trenham of the horror of his solitary state. Wharton also makes lavish use of ellipses, sentence breaks, and periods of silence—techniques that appeared less often in her early tales—to convey the intensity of their distress.

The six tales analyzed in Chapter 2 portray "prisoners of consciousness" who find themselves hopelessly trapped in love and marriage. Several of these men and women, like Mindon in "The Line of Least Resistance" and Nalda Craig in "Permanent Wave," attempt to escape their imprisoned state; however, they are "too late" to free themselves from their marital prisons. Others, like Delia Corbett in "The Lamp of Psyche" and Lizzie West in "The Letters," participate in their own imprisonment by yielding to standards of morality that others invoke.

In her early tales of love and marriage, Wharton introduces a number of narrative techniques to present her theme of imprisonment. Dramatic irony dominates her characterizations of the not-so-admirable spouses of her imprisoned protagonists, and scathing satire repeatedly surfaces in her pointed references to the vacuous upper-class society to which these troubled victims belong. Especially provocative are the beginnings of several of the early tales. "Millicent was late—as usual" in "The Line of Least Resistance" and "Thou shalt not be unfaithful—to thyself" in "The Reckoning" support Wharton's belief that the opening lines of a short story provide the "germ of the whole" (*WF* 51). Also significant are the telling words and phrases that provide sign-posts for her theme of imprisonment; symbolic settings, particularly the image of the house and the rooms within, that present a "metaphor of self" (Wolff 65); and striking eye imagery that reveals the innermost thoughts of Wharton's entrapped central characters.

In her later tales of love and marriage, Wharton employs many of these same techniques, albeit more prominently than before. Irony and satire play a major role in the characterizations of her protagonists, and images of imprisonment become more numerous and more explicit. However, most important, Wharton makes use of a number of stylistic devices that reveal the inner consciousness of her trapped sensibilities. Imagery of the heart and hands is added to that of the eyes; "vital dialogue" signals "the significant passages of their [Wharton's characters'] talk" (*BG* 203), and time shifts, most notably the flashback, reveal events of the past that shed light and significance on the present. Interior monologues, too, record the mental and visual reactions of her protagonists. In "The Letters" and "Permanent Wave," in particular, Wharton extends each monologue in order to present her central characters "alone and unguarded—even by the censoring Self" (Macauley and Lanning 89).

In her early and later tales of love and marriage, therefore, Wharton presents men and women who are the entrapped "victims of an innate disharmony between love and response, need and capacity" (Howe 15), and through the diverse and innovative techniques she employs, her theme of imprisonment is manifestly and dramatically revealed.

Chapter Three

Prisoners of Society _____

Edith Wharton made use of a number of metaphors when discussing the modern short story. In *The Writing of Fiction*, for example, she defines the short story as "a shaft driven straight into the heart of human experience" (36). This metaphor aptly describes the six stories examined in this chapter: they are shafts driven into the hearts of men and women imprisoned by the dictates of society. In these stories, two of Wharton's central characters resentfully endure society's rejection, two deliberately provoke society's condemnation, and two reluctantly submit to society's conventions. As in Chapter 2, three tales from Wharton's early period, "Mrs. Manstey's View," "A Cup of Cold Water," and "Friends," are paired with three from her major or late periods, "Duration," "The Bolted Door," and "The Pretext," in order to illustrate her thematic and technical development.[1]

In her early tales of prisoners of society, as in her early tales of love and marriage, Wharton continues to employ symbolic settings, in particular, the enclosed space to symbolize lives locked in by society's demands. Irony also figures prominently in Wharton's characterizations of society's "prisoners of consciousness": Mrs. Manstey in "Mrs. Manstey's View," Woburn in "A Cup of Cold Water," and Penelope Bent in "Friends" react in ways

_____

1. The material on "Mrs. Manstey's View" and "Duration" appeared in "Images of Imprisonment in Two Tales of Edith Wharton" in the *College Language Association Journal* 36 (March 1993): 318–26 and is reprinted with the permission of the editor.

contrary to those expected of them. And, occasionally, Wharton introduces satire in her descriptions of the "forms of elegance" (1: 153) preoccupying the artificial upper-class society that all too often entraps her vulnerable central characters.

Most important, in these early tales of prisoners of society, Wharton experiments with several techniques that were not discussed in her early tales of love and marriage in Chapter 2. In "A Cup of Cold Water," for example, she introduces a tale-within-a-tale in order to provide a guilt-ridden embezzler with "a vehicle for self-discovery" (Wolff 157). In "Mrs. Manstey's View" and "Friends," she employs the framing device to drama-tize the inability of two disillusioned victims to escape their imprisoned state. She also makes use of nature's elements—the rain in "Mrs. Manstey's View," the ice and frost in "A Cup of Cold Water," and the spring mud in "Friends"—to reinforce the theme of imprisonment.

In her later tales of prisoners of society, Wharton once again makes lavish use of satire in her graphic descriptions of the preoccupations of the rich: the Warbeck ball in "Duration" and the Higher Thought Club in "The Pretext" provide the occasions for her vitriolic jabs. Moreover, she contin-ues to employ dramatic time shifts and eye-opening interior monologues to reveal the innermost thoughts and feelings of her entrapped protagonists. And, as before, images of imprisonment—locked hands, bolted doors, and ticking clocks—are recurrent symbols.

But, as with the early tales, Wharton employs a number of artistic devices that have not been previously examined. Names become significant. She tells us that "my characters always appear with their names. Sometimes these names seem to me affected, sometimes almost ridiculous; but I am obliged to own that they are never fundamentally unsuitable" (*BG* 201). Hence, the surnames of Martha Little in "Duration" and Margaret Ransom in "The Pretext" may seem at first "almost ridiculous" in that they bear little resemblance to the manner in which these characters behave; nonetheless, they enhance Wharton's ironic characterizations and highlight her impris-onment theme. The physiognomy of her protagonists also figures promi-nently in these late tales. The resentful eyes in "Duration," sweaty foreheads in "The Bolted Door," and flushed faces in "The Pretext" help mirror the emotional turmoil of the men and women victimized by society.

"Mrs. Manstey's View" (1891), the first of Edith Wharton's published tales, introduces into her fiction the enclosed space and "the trapped sensibility," thematically presaging almost all of her stories that follow. "The thematic use of enclosed space—a house, a garden, a room, even a valley—," Cynthia Griffin Wolff points out, "can be found throughout

Wharton's mature work in the most subtle and suggestive variations" (64). In this early tale, Wharton portrays Mrs. Manstey as an elderly semi-invalid entrapped in the third-floor back room of a New York City boardinghouse. Irony marks Wharton's characterization of this usually "uncommunicative" (1: 3) recluse who speaks out boldly against an extension that will shut out the life-giving view from her window. Ultimately she opts for death rather than accept society's prison. Most important, Wharton frames the narrative to dramatize the fixed position of her helpless victim.

The tale opens with Mrs. Manstey seated at her favorite window, transfixed by the blossoming scenery that "surrounded and shaped her life as the sea does a lonely island" (1: 5). Significantly, Wharton interjects subtle images of imprisonment in her description of the view that affords her protagonist such pleasure:

> Mrs. Manstey, from her coign of vantage (a slightly projecting bow window where she nursed an ivy and a succession of unwholesome-looking bulbs), looked out first upon the yard of her own dwelling, of which, however, she could get but a restricted glimpse. Still, her gaze took in the topmost boughs of the ailanthus below her window, and she knew how early each year the clump of dicentra strung its bending stalk with hearts of pink. (1: 4)

Clearly, the "projecting bow window" with its "restricted glimpse" of the yard below and nature's images—the ivy that needs nursing, the "unwholesome-looking bulbs," the "bending stalk" of the dicentra—reflect this poor widow's restricted life.

Wharton also notes the depressing images outside Mrs. Manstey's window that reflect her dismal existence—the "stony wastes" strewn with "broken barrels," "empty bottles," "paths unswept"; the "neglected syringa, which persisted in growing in spite of the countless obstacles opposed to its welfare" (1: 4); the many changes of color signaling the passage of another season; the leafless boughs. "Wharton had an intense visual awareness, especially of nature—a sensitivity she shares with many of her characters" (29), Marilyn French tells us, and in her first tale, Wharton exploits this visual awareness to reinforce her imprisonment theme. Particularly significant is the "black lattice of branches against a cold sulphur sky at the close of a snowy day" (1: 5), an image strikingly symbolic of the imprisonment Wharton's elderly protagonist endures inside her lonely room.

For Mrs. Manstey has led a solitary existence the past seventeen years, the reader is told, because her husband died, and her only daughter married and moved to California. Now she and her daughter exchange infrequent "perfunctory letters" (1: 3), and her few acquaintances rarely come to visit.

Her only real friends are the "denizens of the yards" (1: 5), the plants and animals that she is able to see each day from her window.

In fact, when the narrative begins, Mrs. Manstey is scrutinizing the magnolia in "the very next enclosure" (1: 4)—an image symbolic of Mrs. Manstey herself. To her dismay, she is interrupted by a visit from Mrs. Sampson, her landlady. As she removes herself from the window with "ladylike resignation" (1: 5), she remarks that the magnolia is blossoming earlier this year, an observation that foreshadows her own bursting forth by the story's end. But her landlady does not share her interest in the magnolia in the next yard. She is not even aware of its existence. She has come to inform Mrs. Manstey that their next-door neighbor, Mrs. Black (an appropriate name considering the depressing effect her revelation has on Wharton's protagonist), is building an extension "right up to the roof of the main building" (1: 6).

Mrs. Manstey pales as she realizes that this towering addition will completely block the view that gives her life meaning. The wisteria and horse chestnut outside her window will soon bloom again, but she will not be able to see them: "Between her eyes and them a barrier of brick and mortar would swiftly rise" (1: 6), a startling image dramatizing the prison-like existence of this lonesome shut-in.

The natural elements—rain, "the slanting gray gauze" of the sky, and the "bat-colored dusk" (1: 6)—parallel Mrs. Manstey's somber mood the day following Mrs. Sampson's announcement. Painfully despondent, Wharton's protagonist considers moving, but she is unable to envision her life without her shabby room and the view that sustains her. Despite its stained wallpaper, torn carpet, and musty books, her room is like a second skin to her, an outer covering that provides her only refuge, and she compares leaving it to being "flayed alive" (1: 7). She knows she simply would not survive.

She decides, therefore, to call on her next-door neighbor to plead that the extension not be built. Although Wharton portrays Mrs. Manstey at the beginning of the tale as lacking "the power of expression"—the ability to give "utterance to her feelings had she wished to" (1: 5)—she now describes her protagonist courageously speaking out against the extension:

> "I am a poor woman, Mrs. Black, and I have never been a happy one. . . . I never had what I wanted. . . . For years I wanted to live in the country. I dreamed and dreamed about it; but we never could manage it. . . . Then my husband died and I was left alone. That was seventeen years ago. I went to live at Mrs. Sampson's and I have been there ever since. I have grown a little infirm, as you see, and I don't get out often; only on fine days, if I am feeling

very well. So you can understand my sitting a great deal in my window." (1: 7–8)

This poignant outpouring of emotion bespeaks the extent of Mrs. Manstey's distress. Nonetheless, Mrs. Black remains unmoved. Only when her usually reticent neighbor suddenly grabs her by the wrist with her stiff, gout-ridden hand and screams that she does not want to move does Mrs. Black fearfully acquiesce to her plea and falsely promise that she will put a stop to the work on the extension.

But Mrs. Manstey has been deceived. She awakens the following day to find that the work has begun. Feeling like the "ignored magnolia" (1: 6) in its enclosed space, she sits at her customary place by the window, painfully watching as the bricks begin to multiply on the extension.

At this crucial point in the narrative, Wharton introduces a remarkable little scene to parallel symbolically her protagonist's plight. One of the men working below Mrs. Manstey's window picks a magnolia blossom, smells it, and throws it away. Almost immediately, he is followed by another worker who "[treads] on the flower in passing" (1: 9). Like the discarded blossom, Wharton's central character also feels plucked, tossed aside, and crushed by society's dictates.

Her anguish is ameliorated, however, when, after overhearing a workman complain about the dangerous accumulation of paper and rubbish on the building site, she decides to set fire to the "barrier of brick and mortar" that is obliterating the only beauty remaining in her imprisoned life.

That night, with an abandon not unlike that of the "wild wind" that is "blotting the stars with close-driven clouds" (1: 9)—Wharton makes ample use of nature to provide yet another powerful image of imprisonment—Mrs. Manstey secures a kettle of kerosene from the closet and unlocks her door in order to proceed to the dark basement of her boardinghouse. There she unlocks another door, "the iron door" (1: 10) to the yard, and steps out into the cold night air, temporarily freeing herself from the prison of her room.

Although the fire does little damage to Mrs. Black's house, Mrs. Manstey's "little mischief" (1: 10) has serious results. Unable to endure even a brief separation from her life-sustaining room, she becomes ill with pneumonia. Realizing that death is near, she whispers feebly that she wishes to be lifted out of bed so that, like the slumbering magnolia tree, she can catch an early glimpse of the sun's golden rays.

Fated to spend her final moments propped at her favorite window, Mrs. Manstey dies a short time before the work resumes that will remove the view she deemed so "full of interest and beauty" (1: 3). Wharton's description of her entrapped protagonist dying with a smile on her face contains a final irony: rather than accept society's latest rejection, Mrs. Manstey has courageously chosen to die at her special window with "all her radiant world" (1: 6).

Forty-five years later, Wharton wrote "Duration" (1936), a late tale with an analogous story line and theme. Martha Little, a centenarian, has also suffered the cold indifference of her relatives for a long time. Like Mrs. Manstey, she lives alone, in a "dingy little house" (2: 865) that was bequeathed to her at Frostingham, an appropriate name considering the frostlike treatment she has received from her upper-class family. Possessing neither money nor stylish dress, nor even a bad temper (an ironic touch considering the end of the story), advantages that might lift her out of "her congenital twilight" (2: 859), she remains virtually a prisoner in her enclosed space. And because she has "weak eyes," she lives "with the blinds down" (2: 859), a subtle image of enclosure that mirrors her imprisoned life.

Although thematic parallels may be drawn between "Mrs. Manstey's View" and its later counterpart, significant differences can be found in the techniques Wharton employs. In the early tale, symbolic settings define Wharton's protagonist: the neglected syringa and ignored magnolia are metaphors for the lonely shut-in. In "Duration," setting plays a lesser role. Wharton refers to setting only once, when she contrasts her central character's dingy house with the more comfortably furnished residence of her wealthy relatives. Instead, in this late tale, dramatic irony and scathing satire are Wharton's weapons. Both appear in the pretentious conversations of Miss Little's socially prominent family. Irony also figures in Wharton's use of the name Little and her repetition of the word "small." Neither diminutive accurately describes her protagonist, who demonstrates that despite her name, her little house, and her "small figure" (2: 864), she is not as "effaced, contourless, colorless" (2: 859) as her upper-class family believes. She may possess "a small reedy voice" and "a small mottled face" (2: 865), but by the tale's end, she rebels against society's rejection more successfully than her predecessor.

As the tale begins, Henley Warbeck, Martha Little's cousin, is returning home to attend his relative's hundredth birthday celebration. Bewildered by the notoriety this event is occasioning, he mulls over the infamous escapade that resulted in his cousin's ostracism by her family. Years before, he recalls, Cousin Martha "overstepped the line thus drawn for her" (2: 860) by committing a "glaring indelicacy" (2: 861): she had the effrontery to attend the fancy coming-out Warbeck ball dressed in "the prim black silk, the antiquated seed pearls and lace mittens, the obvious 'front,' more tightly crimped than usual," with "an absurd velvet reticule over her wrist" (2: 861). She embarrassed her wealthy relatives further when she unabashedly mingled with "the jeweled and feathered throng under the wax candles of the many chandeliers" until the last guests departed and "the last candle was blown out" (2: 861). Wharton's satire, as she describes the lavish ball and its devastating effect on her protagonist, "indicated her own disposition: her impatience with stupidity and affectation and muddy confusion of mind and purpose" (Van Doren 278).

Martha Little was never allowed to forget her "indelicate" behavior the night of the ball. Her annual seaside invitation as companion to Mrs. Warbeck was revoked, and she was "more and more forgotten" (2: 859) by her large family. Only when there was a sick child to care for or some other household emergency to attend to was she summoned. When the crisis passed, she was again relegated to oblivion. As the number of family emergencies diminished, she, like Mrs. Manstey, "vanished into a still deeper twilight" (2: 862).

However, now that Martha is approaching her hundredth birthday and is enjoying celebrity status in Frostingham, her relatives' reminiscences about the infamous ball and the seed pearls that she wore that fateful night are quite changed. Now they label the affair "that wonderful ball of Grandma's" (2: 863), forgetting their previous displeasure and repudiation of their poor cousin. Now Martha's "antiquated seed pearls," the "funny old ornaments that everybody laughed at" at the ball (2: 863), are, ironically, considered heirlooms. (Wharton uses seed pearls, the tiniest pearls, to reinforce her ironic characterization of the diminutive Miss Little.) Even the press refers to them reverentially as "the Wrigglesworth pearls" (2: 868). Yet these now "priceless" pearls contributed in part to Cousin Martha's years of rejection by her socially prominent family.

Warbeck's subsequent visit with Cousin Martha in her "small square parlor" (2: 865)—Wharton's imprisonment imagery is prominent here—reveals that her involuntary isolation has destroyed neither her mind nor her spirit. In fact, her hundredth birthday celebration seems to have resulted in a kind of rebirth for "the Crown Jewel of the clan" (2: 865). Warbeck is taken aback when his centenarian relative informs him of her unusual pursuits. He finds her boasting about her faddish hairdo, morning massage, and upcoming plane ride both ironic and amusing. As Patricia R. Plante points out, "Edith Wharton's use of irony had always been the method best suited to both her purpose and talent in communicating humor" (368). And irony and humor also appear in Wharton's comic description of Martha's "mummied" hand, "tast[ing] like an old brown glove that had been kept in a sandalwood box" (2: 865), especially in light of its animated handiwork at the conclusion of the tale.

But Miss Little not only boasts of her achievements to Warbeck. She also acknowledges her bitter resentment of Cousin Syngleton Perch, who has intruded on her celebration, alleging at the last minute that he, too, is a centenarian. Although she begrudgingly concedes that he is one of "our own people" (2: 866), she is unable to forget the painful years of rejection she has endured at the hands of those same people.

The following day, therefore, when Perch totters into an informal rehearsal of the hundredth birthday celebration supported by "his elderly Antigone"—Wharton's penchant for classical allusion surfaces here—his Cousin Martha's greeting is caustic and critical: "Well, you really *are* a hundred, Syngleton Perch; there's no doubt about that. . . . And I wonder whether you haven't postponed your anniversary a year or two?" (2: 866). Yes, Martha Little is still smarting from her past humiliation, and she wants her cousin to know that she is not unaware of his present deception.

Consequently, when she sees him nearing the seat next to her on the makeshift platform that has been set up, she antagonistically explodes: "No, no! This is the Bishop's!" (2: 868), adding, "It's *my* rehearsal, isn't it?" (2: 869). After so many years of involuntary seclusion, she has become quite possessive of the spotlight and is incensed at the thought of a "co-divinity" (2: 868) seated at her side. However, Perch, ironically named because Martha Little has no intention of allowing him the elevated position his name suggests, also becomes enraged when he discovers that he is not seated center stage next to his cousin. He fumes that he is not mentioned on the gold-headed commemorative cane she will be presented by the Frostingham selectmen the following day. But Martha remains unforgiving: she will not allow him to share her celebrity.

She pretends to placate him, however, cunningly suggesting that he escort her from the platform when the rehearsal concludes. As he approaches, she makes an "unexpected movement" (2: 871) that places her commemorative cane in his path. And, as she had hoped, Perch falls with a crash.

During the uproar that follows, Warbeck—who suspects that his cousin's movement may have been deliberate—fears she will be distraught by the shock of what has occurred. However, he is in error. Indeed, Wharton makes use of a plethora of negatives to emphasize how guiltless Miss Little feels after Perch's fall: she remains "motionless and untrembling" with "her countenance unmoved" (2: 871). The same mettle she displayed years before at the Warbeck ball sustains her now. As the narrative concludes, Perch is carried from the platform, and Martha continues to stand "upright" and "unmoved," her eyes surprisingly "resolute" (2: 871).

Although written more than four decades apart, "Mrs. Manstey's View" and "Duration" contain several striking similarities in story line and theme.

Both victims are elderly women. Both were ignored by family and friends. And both spent years trapped in their prison cells—the shabby back room of a New York boardinghouse and the dingy little house at Frostingham— prior to carrying out their "rebellious" acts. However, Wharton's treatment of her protagonists' response to society's rejection is quite different. In the early tale, Mrs. Manstey opts to die with a smile on her face before the view that sustained her locked-in existence is forcibly taken away. In the later tale, one of the few Wharton tales in which the imprisoned protagonist acts as avenger, Martha Little successfully rebels against the years of rejection by emerging from her involuntary isolation a tyrannical giant.

Wharton also introduces a variety of the same techniques—symbolic settings, irony, satire, even unusual names—to spotlight her protagonists' imprisoned lives. But perhaps her most notable technical achievement in the later tale is her deft handling of the flashback and interior monologue. In "Mrs. Manstey's View," the omniscient narrator's brief history at the beginning of the tale and Mrs. Manstey's few lines to Mrs. Black furnish scanty details about the background of Wharton's protagonist. In "Duration," however, Warbeck's illuminating interior monologue reveals incidents from the past that enable the reader to understand Martha Little's vindictive response to Cousin Syngleton Perch's intrusion. Furthermore, this backward look recalls the infamous ball when Cousin Martha first displayed her extraordinary mettle, thus preparing the way for the "glaring indelicacy" (2: 861) that ends the tale. Of course, Wharton's irony in the later tale is especially delicious. Feisty old Martha Little secures "a century of slow revenge" with an "abrupt gesture" and an "ancient smile" (2: 871).

"A Cup of Cold Water" (1899), a tale written during Wharton's early period, also describes the imprisonment of an individual by society. However, in this narrative, Wharton focuses on an impoverished cashier in a prominent New York banking house who attempted, unsuccessfully, to overcome the societal restrictions poverty imposes. Woburn has been burned (as his name implies) by his dream of the glamorous lifestyle of the rich. He committed a criminal act—embezzlement—in order to satisfy its extravagant demands.

Consistent with Wharton's belief that "the artist depends on atmosphere for the proper development of his gift" (*WF* 64), setting once again plays a major role in defining character in this early tale. The "sleety rain" (1: 156) and "pools in the pavement . . . stiffening into ice" (1: 151) at the beginning of the narrative mirror Woburn's numbing inability to accept responsibility for his crime, and the "early sunshine" and "tranquil air" (1: 170–71) at the end signal his gradual awakening to "a new phase of consciousness" (1:

169). Irony also highlights Wharton's characterization of Woburn, who, in
his attempt to escape the limitations of his shabby existence, secures for
himself more restrictive surroundings. And, as in "Duration," Wharton's
sophisticated satire repeatedly lashes out at the preoccupations of the rich,
whose pretentious lives have all the earmarks of "a domino party at which
the guests were forbidden to unmask" (1: 157). Finally, Wharton experiments with a tale-within-a-tale—a relatively uncommon artistic device in
her early narratives—to expedite her protagonist's ultimate decision "to face
the future" (1: 171) with his integrity restored.

Wharton's early tale begins as Woburn wends his way along Fifth Avenue
in the early hours of a cold, frosty morning. He turns up the collar of his
Alaskan sable-lined coat and puts his hands deep into his pockets, hoping
to pass unnoticed on his last day in New York. His dream of a life of luxury
has been shattered, and he has decided to make a hasty exodus from the city
to escape the inevitable retribution awaiting him. The "dry blast" (1: 151)
of air searing his face suggests his desiccated thinking, and the frost and ice
forming on the pavement mirror his hardened spirit.

At this point in the narrative, Wharton enters into the consciousness of
her central character to explain why he has decided to take "a cold voyage"
(1: 151) the following day. In an extended flashback, she chronicles his
innermost thoughts on the catastrophic events leading to his present predicament. Months before, Woburn recalls, he began his pursuit of Miss
Talcott, a beautiful, wealthy young socialite. Wharton's splendid satire
surfaces in her powerful description of the desirable Miss Talcott and the
young women in her fashionable social set. She mocks their "skillfully-
rippled hair and skillfully-hung draperies" and the hours they while away
"participating in the most expensive sports, eating the most expensive food
and breathing the most expensive air" (1: 152).

Nonetheless, Woburn found Miss Talcott's lifestyle most attractive. His
own life had been so plagued with tragedy—his father lost his fortune and
died leaving his wife and children penniless—that he was readily seduced
by "the luminous atmosphere where life was a series of peaceful and
good-humored acts, unimpeded by petty obstacles" (1: 153). Although he
now acknowledges the "artificiality" of Miss Talcott's material possessions
and the "audacious irrelevance" (1: 153) of her frivolous ideas, at the time
he met her he was so taken with her affluent lifestyle that he resolved he
would become a rich man in order to marry her.

Sadly, this decision marked the beginning of Woburn's imprisonment. To
impress the desirable Miss Talcott, he spent money recklessly on a sable-
trimmed overcoat, theater tickets, flowers, cab fares, charitable contributions—extravagances he felt were required to win her. And since his

relationship was progressing so smoothly, he foolhardily continued to live "the illusion of unlimited credit" (1: 153). Because his debts multiplied, he borrowed money from the firm until he had spent an entire year's salary in a few months' time. Wharton is blatantly ironic when she reveals that Woburn, in an attempt to escape permanently the "bad food, ugly furniture, complaints and recriminations" (1: 153) of his poverty-stricken state, began embezzling and eventually cheated his banking firm out of fifty thousand dollars. Hence, if he remains in town, he will be returned to those "mean conditions" (1: 153)—albeit in prison—he tried so hard to escape.

Woburn's delving into the past continues as he recalls his trek through the sleet earlier that evening. He remembers heading for the Gildermere ball, hopeful that he would catch a final glimpse of his lost love. He also remembers rushing past familiar landmarks and seeing street people for the very first time—the pitiful beggar hiding in the shadows, the drunken woman squatting on a doorstep. Wharton introduces these unfortunates into her central character's consciousness to awaken in him the realization that despite his expensive attire, he is, in fact, no better off than they. They are all victims of society's rejection, imprisoned in their failed lives.

Woburn also remembers the feelings of failure and rejection he experienced when he arrived at the glamorous ball. The "shining parquet," "white skirts," and "flying tulle" (1: 158)—mesmerizing externals that contributed to his fall from grace—evoked a sudden awareness that the people circling the dance floor were also like strangers. He could not believe that he once considered them his friends. Wharton's description of the upper-class men and women who until now had been so attractive to Woburn smarts with blistering satire: "these mincing women, all paint and dye and whalebone, these apathetic men who looked as much alike as the figures that children cut out of a folded sheet of paper" (1: 156). Watching them, he realized how foolish he had been: these painted women and spiritless men were not as close to him as the derelict and the drunk on the street. At least he was linked to the street people "by the freemasonry of failure" (1: 157).

Moreover, when he observed his former associates at the ball, he realized, painfully, that the men dancing by had accumulated their wealth by devious means and that the women accompanying them were not interested in how the money was acquired. They only wanted to marry these men and ensnare others like them for their daughters. Ironically, he queried: "Was it to live among such puppets that he had sold his soul? What had any of these people done that was noble, exceptional, distinguished? . . . Who were they, that they should sit in judgment on him?" (1: 156). He even hypothesized that if he returned in ten years a wealthy man, his indiscretion would be overlooked. Once again, Wharton enters into the consciousness of her protagonist to deliver another satiric jab at the hypocritical morality of upper-class society:

> Was not all morality based on a convention? What was the stanchest code of ethics but a trunk with a series of false bottoms? Now and then one had the illusion of getting down to absolute right or wrong, but it was only a false bottom—a removable hypothesis—with another false bottom underneath. There was no getting beyond the relative. (1: 157–58)

Woburn's recollection of the happenings earlier in the evening ends abruptly when he suddenly decides to go to a hotel to endure the few hours left before dawn. Going to the steamer that night would be too dismal, too oppressive. He desires a less stifling atmosphere where he will not feel so entrapped by guilt, where he will not feel imprisoned in the consciousness of the shameful crime he has committed.

The second section of Wharton's tale begins when Woburn enters the hotel, and "a wave of dry heat" (1: 159), not unlike the dry wind that blasted him outside, blows into his face—a reminder to the reader that his thinking remains dried up and unproductive. Noticing that he is luggageless, the night clerk remarks ironically, "This one's been locked out" (1: 159). In truth, Woburn's wrongdoing has already locked him into an imprisoned state.

Not surprisingly, Wharton makes use of Woburn's hotel stay to awaken the voice of conscience in her protagonist. After climbing the three flights to his room, he heads down a passageway lined with boots that remind him of his imminent getaway from "yesterday's deeds" (1: 159). A blurred mirror above the dressing table confirms what the reader already knows: his vision is distorted. As he looks out the window, a series of depressing images confront him. The dimly lighted "forsaken thoroughfare," "the lonely figure of a policeman," "the abandoned sidewalks" (1: 160) mirror his feelings of alienation and abandonment. He yearns for sleep to numb his pain but fears missing his boat.

The sounds of a woman sobbing uncontrollably in the next room contribute to his grief. When her tears subside and he hears the unmistakable click of a pistol, he moves quickly to prevent her from pulling the trigger. Pleading that he is "a man who has suffered enough to want to help others" (1: 162), he persuades her to tell him the reason for her despair. She reveals that she betrayed her husband, a telegraph operator on the railroad, by running off with a fascinating traveling salesman who, she later discovered, was already married. Angrily she admits that the salesman charmed her with stories of New York society life, and she became "like somebody in a trance" (1: 164). With her contrived tale-within-a-tale, Wharton has begun to parallel the entrapped Woburn and the suicidal woman. Both were be-witched by New York society life, and both were "in a trance" when they committed their shameful acts.

This desperate victim tells Woburn that she would like to express her remorse to her husband, but, unfortunately, she has no money to return home. Conveniently, Woburn volunteers to pay her hotel bill and buy her a train ticket home. In response, she compares him to her husband—"the best man I've ever seen. . . . a real hero" (1: 167)—and recounts a time when her husband voluntarily confessed to a negligent act: "And I'm sure you'd behave just like him. . . . You'd never do a mean action, but you'd be sorry for people who did; I can see it in your face; that's why I trusted you right off" (1: 168). Now Wharton purposefully compares her protagonist with the stranger's husband to provide the necessary motivation for Woburn to confess his crime and free himself from his guilt-filled consciousness.

The young woman's words certainly affect Woburn. Walking to the window, he pulls up the shade—a symbol of his mounting awareness—and suggests they look out the window to watch the sunrise. Wharton's exquisite description of the beginning of a new day aptly mirrors the awakening of Woburn's moral consciousness: "The light came gradually . . . it seemed to him that he was returning to some forgotten land" (1: 168–69).

A number of symbolic images also signal metaphorically the conversion that has occurred in Woburn. Wharton portrays him turning up the collar of his fur coat to hide the last vestiges of his entrapment in the glamorous lifestyle of the rich. She notes the "fresh blast of heat" (1: 169)—unlike the dry blast that blew at him at the beginning of the narrative—as he leaves the room. And she describes his breakfast in an "unventilated coffee room" (1: 170): stale rolls, stale butter, and a cup of tea made with cold water are grim reminders of the "mean conditions" he will soon be forced to endure.

Once outside, he observes the hurrying cars, shopgirls, and schoolchil-dren, signs that the city, like him, has awakened to a new day. He walks the same path down Fifth Avenue that began the narrative, and when he arrives at his rooms again, he is greeted by friendly images—a burning fire and cheerful books and photos. Only the remains of letters from Miss Talcott in the fireplace ashes remind him that he has repudiated his past fascination with the frivolous concerns of the upper class. As the tale concludes, he steps out into the sunshine and hastens toward the private offices of his employer. Although painfully aware of what lies ahead, for a brief moment "he carried his head high, and shunned no man's recognition" (1: 171).

Lewis, in his biography of Edith Wharton, reveals that in 1894 Wharton's editor at Scribner's rejected "A Cup of Cold Water," terming it "wildly improbable" (81). Wharton subsequently reworked it, and five years later the tale was published. Nonetheless, much of the second part of this two-part tale is as Wharton's editor labeled it. The timely appearance of the suicidal woman in the room adjoining Woburn's, who just happens to be in a tragic situation remarkably parallel to his, is clearly melodramatic, and the story of her high-principled husband's voluntary and gratuitous confession of wrongdoing in order to effect a similar response in Woburn does render the tale improbable.

Moreover, the tale-within-a-tale does seem to contradict Wharton's assertion that an incident in a story "cannot but be fringed with details more and more remotely relevant, and beyond that with an outer mass of irrelevant facts" (*WF* 9). But obviously Wharton has introduced these seemingly irrelevant details to bring about her protagonist's return to an honorable state. In this regard, Elizabeth Hardwick points out, Wharton "is often caught up in contrivance as a furtherance of product" (28). Both Woburn and the suicidal woman are victims, and it is as a result of their contrived meeting that their victimization is addressed.

Of course, as in several of Wharton's other early tales—"The Lamp of Psyche" and "The Line of Least Resistance"—the transformation that occurs in her protagonist is swift and unexplained. Although it is clear that Woburn sympathizes with the strange woman's story, Wharton fails to reveal what prompts him to cancel his trip and confess his crime. The narrator makes only a brief but revealing disclosure: "He had no thought of flight" (1: 171). With this succinct aside and the movement from images that held Woburn frozen in his guilt-ridden consciousness—the restrictions (and constrictions) of the cold and ice—to images of warmth—the "new aroma of coffee" and the "fresh blast of heat"—the reader is made aware that Woburn is returning to the "forgotten land" of responsible conduct.

"The Bolted Door" (1910), the companion tale to "A Cup of Cold Water," was written at the height of Wharton's major phase. Significantly, this suspense-filled tale contains a strikingly symbolic title and the memorable phrase "prisoner of consciousness" (2: 23), which Lewis defines as "entrapment . . . within one's own mental skin" (253). Indeed, Hubert Granice, the central character in this tale, is so entrapped in the prison of his guilt-ridden "mental skin" that he confesses to a murder he committed years before in order to effect society's retribution.

Unlike the early tale, where symbolic settings play a major role, in this late narrative Wharton makes use of setting only when describing the out-of-the-way excursion Granice takes to find someone who will believe his story of murder: "the shabby streets," "basement chophouse," and "twisted trees" (2: 32–33) are metaphors for the depths to which he has sunk. Instead, irony dominates "The Bolted Door." Wharton's characterization of a would-be writer who for years has failed as a playwright because "there isn't enough drama" (2: 5) in his plays is now able, ironically, to recount the story of his crime with so much melodrama that no one believes him. Wharton also pays meticulous attention to time—a technique she employs in the earlier "The Line of Least Resistance," but which she perfects in this late tale—as she traces the beginning of Granice's obsession with becoming a writer to his committing the perfect crime. Finally, as in many of Wharton's later tales, extended interior monologues provide penetrating insights into the guilt-filled consciousness of her imprisoned central character.

The first of Wharton's many references to time dramatically opens the tale. Hubert Granice, "a tired middle-aged man, baffled, beaten, worn out" (2: 3), anxiously awaits the arrival of his attorney, Peter Ascham. He nervously compares the time on his watch to that of the fireplace clock, estimating that his guest will arrive in three minutes and then "there'd be no going back, by God—no going back!" (2: 3). This initial emotional outburst is, to be sure, not uncommon in Wharton's tales. Says Wharton, "It is always a necessity to me that the note of inevitableness should be sounded at the very opening of my tale, and that my characters should go forward to their ineluctable doom" (*BG* 204).

Obviously distraught and entrapped by the restraints of time, Granice becomes unnerved when his servant brings him news that Ascham will not arrive for another thirty minutes. Just as in the beginning of "A Cup of Cold Water," where the protagonist hurries through the streets of New York to allay his feelings of guilt, in the opening scene of "The Bolted Door," Granice paces the length of his library to relieve the tension building within him. Time has become his enemy, and every delay postpones society's sentence for a murder he committed ten years ago.

Throwing himself into a chair, he sits with "locked hands" (2: 4), symbolic of his locked-in existence, before rereading the letter that condemns his latest effort as a playwright. It is no simple rejection letter. This missive advises Granice that the returned manuscript is no more marketable than all the others he has sent—"the thing drags all through"—and that since he has tried writing "all kinds" (2: 5) of plays, perhaps he should consider doing something else. Granice looks back on the past ten years and concludes that half his life has been a failure.

In "A Cup of Cold Water," Wharton never gets into the consciousness of her protagonist to reveal the reasons for his conversion from hardened criminal to repentant sinner, but in this late tale she provides extended interior monologues to involve the reader fully in what Granice is thinking and doing. The workings of his mind, from his dream of becoming a famous

playwright, to the plotting of his cousin's murder, to his current attempts to
convince everyone of his crime, are recorded "just as they come" (*WF* 12).

Granice checks his watch again, but only ten minutes have elapsed since
last he looked. Deeply troubled by the "nightmare of living" (2: 6), he looks
for his revolver and even places it at his head, but decides that "it was of no
use—he knew he could never do it in that way. His attempts at self-destruc-
tion were as futile as his snatches at fame!" (2: 6). He would have to depend
on his revelation to Ascham to rid him of his worthless life.

Another reference to imprisonment follows the dinner with Ascham.
Granice dismisses his servant with the prophetic, "I'll lock up myself" (2:
7). In truth, he is already locked into his guilty conscience. Then, after
initiating a discussion with Ascham on criminals who have never been
apprehended, he suddenly reveals the secret that has tormented him for
years. He tells Ascham he can explain the unsolved murder of his cousin,
Joseph Lenman: "I murdered him—to get his money" (2: 8). In a lengthy
flashback, he pours out the sequence of events that led to the murder ten
years before.

This time shift into the past uncovers a family background remarkably
similar to that of Woburn in "A Cup of Cold Water." Granice reveals that
when he was eighteen, his father died, leaving an enormous debt, and like
Woburn, he was obliged to support both his mother and sister. Detesting his
work in a broker's office, he began to satisfy "his deepest-seated instinct"—
writing plays—which "became a morbid, a relentless obsession" (2: 10).

As the flashback continues, Granice recalls thinking that his wealthy
cousin, Joseph Lenman, might be able to provide an escape from his
loathsome job. He asked for a loan, and when he was callously rejected, he
coldheartedly devised a scheme of murder—poisoning his cousin with one
of this rich man's prized melons—in order to inherit the money Lenman
held in trust for him. An Italian gardener who had been fired by Lenman for
dropping a melon became the prime suspect, but Granice reveals that it was
he who poisoned the melon. And although Wharton's protagonist protests,
ironically, that "I don't want you to think I'm sorry for it. This isn't
'remorse,' understand. . . . I wanted change, rest, *life*, for both of us—
wanted, above all, for myself, the chance to write!" (2: 14), the reader is
aware that his need to confess his crime belies his vehement denial.
Nonetheless, Granice claims to experience no remorse, only regret that his
crime did not produce the outcome he desired.

Ascham listens to Granice for three hours, but believes not a word. A
conversation follows between the attorney and his client that reveals the
extent of Granice's imprisoned consciousness. In sharp contrast to Wharton's early tale, which is punctuated by brief, pointed questions and abbre-

viated responses, "The Bolted Door" is filled with lengthy exchanges that "keep the story steadily moving forward" and "dramatize a series of encounters among the characters . . . to illuminate theme" (Macauley and Lanning 52, 56).

Ascham thinks that his client is depressed because his latest play has been rejected. He even mockingly suggests that Granice may be hallucinating. With this expression of disbelief, Wharton's dramatic irony begins to build. Ascham's response to Granice's incredible but nonetheless factual revelation is certainly ironic. It is ironic, too, that Granice now begins to fear that his attorney will recommend that he be committed to an asylum, which would force him to endure the agony of his failed life indefinitely.

Horrified by these thoughts and still plagued by time and the need to be free of his imprisoned existence, he feels compelled to convince someone else of his story. Despite the hour, he travels a "dim and deserted" (2: 16) avenue, a thoroughfare that mirrors his own darkened state, to reveal his story of murder to his longtime friend and confidant, Robert Denver, editor of the *Investigator*. With the clock on Denver's mantel rhythmically and symbolically ticking away, Granice once more confesses his crime, noting precisely each minute detail of the night he poisoned his cousin.

In this second extended flashback, Wharton, heeding her conviction that the storyteller should try to "feel, see and react" (*WF* 46) as her reflecting mind does, pays particular attention to time. Her protagonist meticulously records the days, hours, and minutes that it took to execute each part of his murderous plan. Hence, the reader begins to appreciate why time has become Granice's enemy. Years before, he could not wait for his dream of a career as a dramatist to be fulfilled. He thwarted time and took another's life. Now, he must defeat time again and hasten his escape from what he perceives as a useless existence.

Ironically, Denver, like Ascham, does not believe the story. He, too, thinks Granice's nerves have "gone to smash" (2: 21) and advises him to see someone who treats individuals with nervous disorders. Granice is crushed. He wished to be convicted of murder, and instead he faces an asylum and a straitjacket. As a result, he becomes more determined to prove his guilt to "some sane impartial mind" (2: 22), someone who does not know him and will expedite the ending of his failed life.

Allonby, the District Attorney, becomes his next victim. Still tormented by the constraints of time, Granice asks to be arrested, but Allonby ironically responds, "Well, I don't know that we need lock you up just yet" (2: 23). But Granice has been "locked up" for some time. A further irony surfaces as Granice departs: Allonby invites him to join him for supper with the actress responsible for the rejection of his latest manuscript.

Following this distressing conversation, Wharton tells us that Granice endured "four days of concentrated horror" (2: 23). And, to enable the reader to appreciate his emotional suffering, she enters into the mind of her central character and delivers one of her most memorable interior monologues on the agony of imprisonment:

> He was chained to life—a "prisoner of consciousness." Where was it he had read the phrase? Well, he was learning what it meant. In the long night hours, when his brain seemed ablaze, he was visited by a sense of his fixed identity, of his irreducible, inexpugnable *selfness*, keener, more insidious, more unescapable, than any sensation he had ever known. He had not guessed that the mind was capable of such intricacies of self-realization, of penetrating so deep into its own dark windings. (2: 23)

Like Woburn, Granice begins to walk the streets to escape his depressing innermost thoughts. He sees people on the street, men who are victimized by their poverty, and realizes, as Woburn does, that they are no different from him. They are all imprisoned in their failed lives, for "the iron circle of consciousness held them too: each one was handcuffed to his own detested ego" (2: 23). He decides that he must take extreme measures to end his imprisoned existence.

With Peter McCarren, a clever young reporter from the *Explorer*, Granice returns to the locale where the murder was planned. Here Wharton resorts to a familiar technique—a symbolic setting—to describe her unstable protagonist as he agonizes over his insoluble dilemma. They survey a "row of tottering tenements and stables" (2: 25), hoping to find the proof necessary to establish that a murder was committed. Unfortunately, they fail. But McCarren's curiosity has been whetted, and he asks Granice why he is suddenly making his crime known. He mentions the word "remorse," and although Granice had previously denied that remorse was his reason for confessing his crime, he now realizes that no one appreciates "craving for death" (2: 27) as a rational motive. He is also aware that while he has never been appreciated for his fictional writings, ironically, everyone, with the possible exception of McCarren, believes that he is weaving a story of murder. The ultimate irony lies in Granice's inability to acknowledge that remorse has indeed prompted his confession of murder. Only a tormented, guilt-ridden mind could reconstruct a crime committed ten years before in such minute detail.

At this point in the narrative, the district attorney sends for the country's most renowned alienist. Granice is horrified. Convinced that Allonby considers him a maniac, he once again fears that a different imprisonment faces him—the walls of an asylum. The alienist, however, tells him that he has "a case of brain fag" and prescribes, ironically, that he find "some larger interest" (2: 30) to take him out of himself. But Granice is so locked into himself that there is no interest large enough to extricate him.

Still obsessed by his compulsion to convince someone of his guilt so that his desire for death can be realized, he begins writing letters to the newspapers to publicize his plight. However, responses from Allonby, Ascham, and Denver revive his fear of being institutionalized, and he decides to discontinue his writing temporarily. Unfortunately, he cannot silence "his inner self" (2: 31): society is locking him into his imprisoned consciousness by thwarting his efforts to end his life. In fact, because "the fixed unwavering desire" (2: 32) to die never leaves him, he even contemplates killing another person to prove he is a murderer.

Instead, he walks the streets to confess his crime to an "impartial stranger" (2: 31) who will believe his story. Here again Wharton makes use of setting—"the bald grass plots and the twisted trees" (2: 33)—to mirror Granice's naked and distorted mind. He ultimately decides to accost a young girl, but as soon as he begins to unburden himself, she runs from him screaming, and he is promptly arrested.

The "large quiet establishment" (2: 33) to which Granice is removed is not what he expected. He had hoped to be arrested for murder. Ironically, such is not the case—he has been institutionalized for a mental disorder. Once more he is tormented by the constraints of time; his inaction becomes "more and more unbearable" (2: 34). Consequently, he recites the details of his crime to his "intelligent companions" (2: 33) in the hope that someone will believe him.

Wharton concludes her tale with its most shocking irony. She recounts an occasion when McCarren and a friend visit Granice. As they leave, the reporter makes a startling revelation: he discovered by accident some time ago that Granice was, in fact, guilty of murdering his cousin. However, he felt that he could not turn him in, so he has remained silent. Ironically, he tells his friend: "Lord, but I was glad when they collared him, and had him stowed away safe in there!" (2: 35). In effect, his silence has condemned Granice to a far worse sentence—now he is imprisoned indefinitely in "the iron circle of consciousness" (2: 23).

The similarities between "A Cup of Cold Water" and its later counterpart are immediately obvious. Both Woburn and Granice became obsessed with the desire for a life different from one that they found intolerable. Consequently, they committed a crime they hoped would effect the change they desired. Sadly, they sentenced themselves to a more painful imprisonment. However, their response to their crimes is very different. Woburn eventually feels remorse and voluntarily returns to accept responsibility for his wrong-doing. Granice remains unable to acknowledge sorrow for his evil act. His only regret is that his entire life has been a failure and that he has been unable to end it.

Several techniques are also common to both tales. As is her custom, Wharton uses verbal irony and symbolic settings to highlight her imprison-ment theme. However, one major difference exists: her execution of the interior monologue. In the early tale, Wharton merges with the conscious-ness of her protagonist only when he reveals the story of his fascination with Miss Talcott and his disenchantment with her wealthy social circle. She never gets into his consciousness to reveal the reasons for his rapid trans-formation. The reader must assume that the conversations in the tale-within-a-tale effected his sudden decision to acknowledge his crime and "face the future" (1: 171) with his head held high. In "The Bolted Door," on the other hand, Wharton does not permit a simple artificially contrived tale-within-a-tale resolution. Instead, she makes use of extended interior monologues throughout the narrative to give the reader penetrating insights into the thoughts and feelings of her obsessed protagonist. Clearly, "the fixed unwavering desire" to die never leaves him—Granice remains a prisoner of consciousness, condemned by society to the life he abhors.

"Friends" (1900), an uncollected story from Wharton's early period, introduces the final set of tales involving men and women imprisoned by the dictates of society. Again, Wharton's pervasive irony figures promi-nently in the tale of Penelope Bent, a middle-aged spinster who left her hometown to marry a traveling salesman, only to discover that he ran off and married another. Irony also characterizes Penelope's relationship with Vexilla Thurber: Wharton's protagonist finds it impossible to reveal the details of her humiliating jilting even to her closest friend. A more subtle irony appears at the tale's end when Penelope, confident she has regained her "old sense of security" (1: 214), once again decides to leave her hometown: in truth, she is still entrapped by public opinion. Wharton also exploits setting in this early tale. Her vivid description of Penelope's hometown and, just as important, her sketch of her protagonist's bedroom enable the reader to appreciate why this staid, well-established school-teacher opted to escape her depressing existence. Finally, like "Mrs. Man-stey's View," "Friends" is framed to emphasize the unchanged emotional state of her imprisoned central character.

Wharton begins her narrative with a lengthy descriptive passage that introduces the reader to the "ugly town" (1: 197) of Sailport. She notes the houses "set apart behind clipped hedges"; the "too narrow" streets "full of snow and mud in winter, of dust and garbage in summer"; "buildings of discordant character"; "wooden wharves and a confusion of masts and smoke-stacks"; "waste spaces strewn with nameless refuse" (1: 197)—images that reflect the sense of hopelessness Wharton wishes to convey. Particularly significant is the line, "Nowhere is there the least peep of green, the smallest open space that spring may use as a signboard" (1: 197). This hopelessness pervades the entire narrative, and, in fact, foreshadows Penelope's continued imprisonment at the tale's end.

In much the same way that Woburn turns up the collar of his sable-lined coat so that he can pass unnoticed on the streets of New York at the beginning of "A Cup of Cold Water," Penelope pulls her hat's "thick veil" (1: 198) over her face as she hurries down Main Street. She, too, hopes to escape the notice of anyone who might recognize her and lowers her eyes to avoid the glances of passersby. Although she acknowledges that her friends would no doubt sympathize with her if they knew of her plight, she would rather die than have them discover what has happened to her. She is so imprisoned in the consciousness of what people will think of her that she shrinks even from the scrutiny of the sunshine" (1: 198).

Nonetheless, despite her feelings of shame, Penelope surveys her "ugly" hometown "with an unexpected sense of relief" (1: 198). She knows that she acted foolishly when she allowed herself to be victimized by a scoundrel, and she is relieved to be home where there are friends she can turn to for sympathy and support. Even though she chooses to avoid seeing anyone she knows, she realizes that she cannot shun the townspeople indefinitely. She must support herself and her ailing mother.

Confident that she can reclaim her former teaching position—the school board had promised they would "put [her] back" (1: 199) should she reconsider her resignation before their next monthly meeting—she hastens to the school building to speak to Mr. Boutwell, a member of the board. Significantly, Wharton endows the building "with an air of moral superiority" (1: 199) in order to reflect Penelope's perception of the judgmental Sailport community.

Indeed, Penelope becomes quite nervous and even tearful in Mr. Boutwell's presence. Although she is usually self-possessed and confident, she is now filled with embarrassment and begins stammering and stuttering. She even glances out the window to avoid his gaze, noting the "blind alley, full of rubbish" (1: 201)—another image signaling her myopic frame of mind.

But Penelope's uneasiness gives way to fury when she learns that her position has been filled by her friend, Vexilla Thurber. She feels betrayed by her friend and deceived by the board, who had for years deemed Vexilla "not 'smart enough' " (1: 200). Only when Mr. Boutwell assures her that Vexilla took the position with the understanding that she would resign should Penelope return does she settle down and acknowledge her confused state. She implores her former superior not to tell anyone that she has returned, not even Vexilla. She is still so possessed by her inordinate concern for how people will judge her that she cannot bear to have those close to her, not even her best friend, know what has happened. Then, fearing his ill will, she reveals the fact of her jilting and proffers an apology for her angry outburst: "I was perfectly hateful about Vexilla when you first told me— perfectly hateful! I don't see how I could behave so.... But the fact is, I'm almost crazy. I don't seem to know what I'm doing—" (1: 204).

Arriving home, Penelope retires to her room and becomes even more dejected. The four walls that formerly provided comfort and security now have "a look of such chill indifference" (1: 205). Even the furniture and once familiar wallpaper repeat, "I know thee not!" (1: 205). In his introduction to Wharton's stories, Lewis points out that rooms and their furnishings are Wharton's "chief source of metaphor in the short stories" (xxi). Clearly Penelope's small bedroom reflects her feelings of utter desolation.

She looks out of the window—Wharton often makes use of the window as a symbol of the desire for escape—and decides she needs a walk in the open air. Still too shame-ridden to reveal her presence to the Sailport community, she retrieves her hat and thick veil and puts them on again. She turns to leave, but not before checking the soil in the geranium plants. Her comment, "It needs loosening" (1: 205), applies to herself as well. With nerves still taut by what she perceives as her disgrace, she cautions her mother as she leaves the house, "If anybody comes in, mother, don't— don't—" (1: 206), a plea that reveals the extent of her distress.

Outside, the falling twilight mirrors Penelope's downcast mood. She is aware of "a growing inability to think" (1: 206), to get beyond the consciousness of her folly, when suddenly she comes face to face with Vexilla, who suggests they visit at her home. Wharton becomes a bit melodramatic—as she is sometimes prone to be in her early tales—when she describes Vexilla's dilapidated house resting on a "strip of down-trodden earth enclosed with broken palings" (1: 208) and the bedroom with its "cracked looking glass and threadbare carpet" (1: 209). (Hence, although Vexilla's name possesses that "excessive oddness" about which Wharton writes, it is a name that is not "fundamentally unsuitable" [BG 201] given her straitened circumstances.) The melodrama continues when Wharton discloses that Vexilla has three dependent relatives—a sickly grandmother, a crippled brother, and a ne'er-do-well sister—all of whom will be left without funds if she leaves her teaching position. Like Penelope, she, too, is an imprisoned victim.

Nonetheless, Vexilla immediately indicates her intention to resign now that her friend has returned: "There's nobody like you—nobody! Oh, it's so good to have you back!" (1: 210). Despite this outpouring of friendship and joy, Vexilla's outburst and her deplorable living quarters sadden Penelope. She bemoans the fact that "life appeared so meaningless and cruel" (1: 209). As Blake Nevius points out, in Wharton's early stories her characters "are intensely aware of one another; they respond to the slightest changes in the atmosphere of thought and sensation conveyed by another presence; and they are equally alive to impressions generated by their physical environment" (34). Penelope is also taken aback by the discovery that the only picture on the wall is a photograph of herself. She is ashamed that she previously misjudged her friend.

More of Wharton's melodrama follows when Vexilla reveals that she has sold her typewriter, the only means by which she previously earned her living. Penelope realizes that there is little chance of her recovering her former teaching position without incurring additional disfavor from those in the community who would sympathize with Vexilla's plight. Consequently, she informs Vexilla that her marriage has only been postponed, that she and her mother will be leaving Sailport for New York. She is still unwilling to reveal the actual reason for her return home and even fabricates a story to justify her imminent departure.

In fact, when Vexilla questions her about leaving Sailport again, Penelope becomes defensive and somewhat belligerent: "You talk as if I didn't know my own mind! I'm not in the habit of saying things I don't mean!" (1: 212). Actually, she is so imprisoned by her perception of what people will think of her that she really is saying things she does not mean. She adjusts her veil over her face as she rises to leave, sending a clear signal that she still suffers from her painful humiliation.

As the tale concludes, Penelope writes a brief note to Mr. Boutwell and once again hurries down Main Street, just as she did at the beginning of the narrative. However, the hesitancy that marked her arrival in Sailport at the beginning of the tale seems gone:

> Now the old sense of security had returned. There still loomed before her, in tragic amplitude, the wreck of her individual hope; but she had escaped from the falling ruins and stood safe, outside of herself, in touch once more with the common troubles of her kind, enfranchised forever from the bondage of a lonely grief. (1: 214)

This sudden revelation, proffered with the perplexing explanation that she had been whirled "through dread spaces of moral darkness and bewilderment" (1: 214) (an explanation remarkably similar to that in "The Line of Least Resistance" when Mindon "felt himself caught in the wheels of his terrific logic, and swept round, red and shrieking, till he was flung off into space" [1: 220]), provides yet another example of the hasty transformations that occur in the protagonists of Wharton's early tales. The disclosure that Penelope feels the "old" security again is made without explanation or justification.

In truth, Wharton's assertion at the conclusion of the narrative that Penelope "stood safe . . . enfranchised forever from the bondage of a lonely grief" belies the actions of her protagonist. Her decision to leave Sailport is evidence that her relation to life has not changed, that the "old sense of security" has not returned, and that she is not free from loneliness and grief. She still believes that the narrow empty streets "deep in spring mud" reflect the Sailport community's "muddy" judgments, and she remains unable to work "her way through the mud" (1: 198). Hence, she remains imprisoned, still entrapped by her continued submission to the standards of the society that she is leaving.

"The Pretext" (1908), a short story written at the beginning of Wharton's major period, recounts the plight of Margaret Ransom, a sexually repressed married woman who remains imprisoned in a marriage and a community characterized by "stolid mediocrity" (Lewis 194). As in "Friends," the tale with which it is paired, irony dominates Wharton's portrayal of this reserved, frustrated matron, who believes that she had been "extraordinarily loved" (1: 649) by a young Englishman until she is told that he used her as "a pretext" (1: 653) to rid himself of an undesirable attachment. Also like "Friends," "The Pretext" is framed, this time with Wharton's protagonist sitting before a mirror, imprisoned by the conventions that society has imposed on her.

However, unlike in "Friends," satire also surfaces—as it typically does in Wharton's later tales—in her brilliant characterization of the aristocratic Wentworth community where Margaret Ransom lives. Just as Sailport's hopeless landscape in "Friends" does not possess even "the least peep of green," Wentworth's standards demand conformity or "obliteration" (1: 636). Wharton also introduces many explicit references to imprisonment: the bolted bedroom door, "dark closet" (1: 638), "winding staircase," and "scant porticoes" (1: 641) are all images that confine and enclose. Finally, interior monologues allow the reader an intimate glimpse into the consciousness of Wharton's protagonist as she moves from her "exquisite illusion" (1: 646) of love to the "unspeakable sadness" (1: 654) of rejection.

The tale begins as Margaret Ransom, the middle-aged wife of the legal representative of Wentworth University, blushes into "the cramped eagle-topped mirror above her plain prim dressing table" (1: 632), images that from the outset echo her restricted life. Because Wharton believed that descriptive passages must always be expressed "within the register" (*WF* 85) of the intelligence involved, she notes those features her central character observes as she studies her reflection in the mirror. Margaret scrutinizes her too thin hair, strained mouth, pale lips, wrinkled eyes, and lined throat, and concludes that she needs some color in her face—and in her life as well: "Relief—contrast—that was it! She had never had any, either in her appearance or in her setting" (1: 633).

Yet she also spies a blush of youth on her face, occasioned by her darting up the narrow stairs to her bedroom after a visit with the young Englishman entrusted to her husband's care. Training to be an electrical engineer, Guy Dawnish has been an almost daily visitor since his arrival in Wentworth a little over a year ago. Although the society of Wentworth ordinarily views such frequent social calls with disfavor, no one deems his visits inappropriate. Margaret conjectures that "she was protected by her age, no doubt—her age and her past, and the image her mirror gave back to her. . . . " (1: 634; Wharton's ellipsis), a judgment that foreshadows the conclusion of the tale. Nonetheless, the blush Margaret Ransom finds so distracting is the result of Dawnish's most recent visit.

Sitting in a "stiff mahogany rocking chair" with her bedroom door bolted, an image mirroring her inflexible New England ancestry, Margaret realizes, as she contemplates her unusual color, that her "perfectly ordered moral consciousness" (1: 633) has been disturbed. She binds a black velvet ribbon around her neck and frizzes her "tight strands of hair" (1: 633)—actions symbolic of her desire to loosen up her rigid life—to provide the momentary relief she so earnestly desires.

Her emotional release, however, is short-lived. Her husband's agitated knock and question, "Why are you locked in?" (1: 634), remind her that she is locked into the social obligations imposed by the Wentworth community. This evening, for example, she is expected to attend a faculty dinner—her husband is the featured speaker—even though she has no wish to go. She is also expected to dress and look like everyone in academe even though, like Melville's Bartleby, she would prefer not to. In fact, her husband's parting gibe at her frizzled mess of hair, "You look like the Brant girl at the end of a tennis match" (1: 635), suggests the conformity, even regarding hairstyle, required of her.

Margaret Ransom attributes her husband's ridicule to his conservative upbringing, an observation that gives Wharton the opportunity to interject a vehement denunciation of the socially exclusive Wentworth community:

The Wentworth "tone" is unmistakable: it permeates every part of the social economy. . . . It sits in judgment not only on its own townsmen but on the rest of the world—enlightening, criticizing, ostracizing a heedless universe— and nonconformity to Wentworth standards involves obliteration from Wentworth's consciousness. (1: 636)

Nonetheless, this Wentworth "tone" has marked the boundaries of Margaret Ransom's life since childhood. Even as she looks out the window in an effort to dismiss the "flushed tumult of sensation" (1: 639) that has unsettled her, the view of the empty "elm-shaded street," "the prim flowerless grass plots," and the "irrelevant shingled gables" (1: 637) symbolically reinforces her feelings of entrapment.

At the faculty dinner that evening, Margaret feels more confined. And when her husband begins his lecture, she finds the atmosphere in the ladies' gallery hot and oppressive, even suffocating. She leaves with Dawnish— who accompanied her to the dinner—for a breath of air, and once again Wharton provides striking images of enclosure—the "shadow of the elms" and the walk down the "lateral path which bent, through shrubberies, toward a strip of turf between two buildings" (1: 641)—to highlight the repression of a woman hemmed in by her conservative ancestry and the Wentworth tone.

Hence, when Dawnish indicates that he has something he must tell her before departing for England, Margaret pleads that he not tell her anything: she feels it is "much safer to leave everything undisturbed" (1: 643). Because she has until now suppressed her passionate feelings for this man, her heart begins to beat wildly at the thought that he may share her deep emotion. Wharton's description of her physical reactions—the rush in her ears, her blushing face, her wildly beating heart—reflects the guilt, even shame, she feels as she strays from those conventions that have thus far kept her emotions under control. Only when she withdraws into her imprisoned consciousness, where her standards remain intact, does she experience relief, coupled with regret: "She had the distinct sensation that her hour— her one hour—was over" (1: 644).

Dawnish leaves Wentworth, and Margaret never sees him alone again. A period of profound loneliness follows, and like John Marcher in James's "The Beast in the Jungle," she feels as though she is the only person who ever lived "to whom *nothing had ever happened*" (1: 646). He does write to her, and she recalls once more her one ecstatic moment by the river; however, as his writing becomes less frequent, she settles back into her prison of "the customary, the recurring" (1: 646). She determines that what for her was a "transformation of her whole being" (1: 646) was for him probably no more than an outpouring of gratitude.

However, about a year later, a letter from abroad leads her to believe that Dawnish shared the "miracle" (1: 646) she experienced that evening by the river and that it had irrevocably altered his life. Upon his return to England, the letter-writer notes, Dawnish broke his engagement to an English heiress, explaining that while he was in America, he "formed an unfortunate attachment" (1: 647). Convinced that she is the unfortunate attachment to whom the letter refers, she suddenly finds new meaning in her mundane life. She becomes especially interested, Wharton reveals satirically, in the architectural studies of the Higher Thought Club—English Gothic becomes her special area of expertise—and she no longer finds her customary duties a burden:

> Her life, thenceforward, was bathed in a tranquil beauty. The days flowed by like a river beneath the moon—each ripple caught the brightness and passed it on. She began to take a renewed interest in her familiar round of duties. The tasks which had once seemed colorless and irksome had now a kind of sacrificial sweetness, a symbolic meaning into which she alone was initiated. She had been restless—had longed to travel; now she felt that she should never again care to leave Wentworth. (1: 649)

A visit from Lady Caroline Duckett, Dawnish's sharp-eyed and sharp-tongued English aunt, however, soon destroys Margaret's illusion that she had been "loved—extraordinarily loved" (1: 649). Demanding to see Mrs. Ransom "at once" (1: 651), Lady Caroline declares, without pausing, that her nephew, Guy, thinks he is in love with her. She adds that he has broken his engagement, adversely affecting a number of people besides himself.

When Margaret indignantly identifies herself several times as the Mrs. Robert Ransom she seeks, Lady Caroline, with a look of "cautious incredulity" (1: 651), tactlessly responds: "I'm so bewildered by this new development—by his using you all this time as a pretext . . . the important thing now is: *who is the woman, since you're not?*" (1: 653). Margaret is stunned by this injudicious question—she smarts at being labeled a pretext.

It is not by accident that Wharton chose the word "pretext." Says Wharton: "I am sometimes startled at the dramatic effect of a word or gesture which would never have occurred to me if I had been pondering over an abstract 'situation,' as yet uninhabited by its 'characters' " (*BG* 204). Indeed, the effect of the word pretext on her protagonist is dramatic. Margaret has been able to tolerate her oppressive life in Wentworth by convincing herself that she had enjoyed a "transcendant [sic] communion"

(1: 649). Now she ponders Dawnish's having used her as "a pretext" and concludes that she has been living in a world of illusion.

The narrative concludes as it began a year before. Margaret Ransom moves from her "pale puritan" (1: 653) drawing room to her bedroom, only instead of springing up the stairs as she did at the beginning of the narrative, she walks slowly and drags her feet up the narrow flight to her room. Symbolically, she bolts the door to her bedroom and looks at herself in the mirror. Now there is no blush on her face. Nor is there any thought to her binding her neck with black velvet or frizzing her hair. She must rid herself of any illusion of youth. Wharton also notes that Margaret looks out the window at the "empty elm-shaded street" (1: 654), just as she had done the year before, to reinforce the unalterable sameness of her protagonist's imprisoned existence. In the penetrating interior monologue that follows, Margaret reflects on her future: "Nothing was changed in the setting of her life, perhaps nothing would ever change in it. She would certainly live and die in Wentworth. And meanwhile the days would go on as usual, bringing the usual obligations" (1: 654).

Having accepted without question Lady Caroline's verdict that she was merely a pretext, used to sever an undesirable attachment, she returns to finish a paper for the Higher Thought Club meeting. In passively acquiescing to one individual's assessment of Dawnish's feelings for her, she participates in her own imprisonment, a long-suffering victim of society's deprecation.

The early "Friends" and later "The Pretext" contain a number of thematic parallels. Two middle-aged women, one married and one single, lead monotonous, colorless lives—Penelope Bent possesses a paleness that suggests "the flatness and premature discoloration of a pressed flower" (1: 198), and Margaret Ransom, by her own admission, is "as flat as the pattern of the wallpaper" (1: 633) in her room. Both women have experienced a jilting, one real and one presumed, and both end the tale where they began. In effect, both remain imprisoned by society's dictates.

To demonstrate that nothing has changed radically for either of her protagonists, Wharton employs a variety of techniques. She makes repeated references to the peculiar features of the landscape—Sailport's "narrow sidewalk" (1: 199) and Wentworth's "elm-shaded street"—to reflect their restrictive surroundings. And she frames her narrative to convey the impression of sameness—as Margaret Ransom observes, "Nothing would ever change in it [her life]."

But "The Pretext" is distinguished by the scathing satire found throughout the tale. Wharton's description of the Wentworth "tone" with "its backward references, its inflexible aversions and condemnations, its hard moral outline preserved intact against a whirling background of experiment" (1: 636) contains one of her strongest indictments of upper-class society. Of course, the Wentworth tone contributes in part to Margaret's more realistic view of her life ahead. In "Friends," Penelope is still running at the tale's end—this time away from Sailport—naively convinced that she has escaped her imprisoned state. Yet her hasty departure from Sailport is evidence that she remains imprisoned by the judgments of the people living in her hometown. In "The Pretext," Wharton's central character still sits in her rocking chair, resigned to remain in the Wentworth community. Unlike Penelope, she is very much aware of the lifelong imprisonment that lies ahead: "She had an aching vision of the length of the years that stretched before her. Strange that one who was not young should still, in all likelihood, have so long to live!" (1: 654).

The six tales examined in Chapter 3 depict individuals who are "prisoners of consciousness" because of the pressures that society has exerted on them. Occasionally, these men and women, like Woburn in "A Cup of Cold Water" and Granice in "The Bolted Door," become so desperate in their attempts to escape their imprisonment that they lock themselves into a different kind of societal control. Others like Mrs. Manstey in "Mrs. Manstey's View" and Martha Little in "Duration," finally liberate themselves of their lifetime of imprisonment, albeit sometimes at a tragic cost.

To present the theme of imprisonment in her early tales of prisoners of society, Wharton employs many of the same techniques found in her early tales of love and marriage. Irony and satire once again emerge in her characterizations of men and women who, in an attempt to escape their restricted lives, ironically return to an imprisoned state. Symbolic settings also recur: the "too narrow" streets (1: 197), "forsaken thoroughfare," and "abandoned sidewalks" (1: 160) in these early tales mirror the psychological prisons of Wharton's central characters. Likewise, Wharton continues to invoke the image of the house and the rooms within as a metaphor for imprisonment. Mrs. Manstey's shabby boardinghouse room, Woburn's dimly lit hotel room, and Penelope Bent's indifferent bedroom reflect lives imprisoned by society's demands.

However, Wharton also experiments with several different techniques in these early tales: a tale-within-a-tale in "A Cup of Cold Water" hastens an entrapped victim's return to "a wholly new phase of consciousness," and the framed narratives in "Mrs. Manstey's View" and "Friends" expose the static condition of Wharton's imprisoned protagonists.

In her later tales of prisoners of society, as in her later tales of love and marriage, irony and satire continue to figure prominently. Extended interior monologues provide illuminating glimpses into the imprisoned consciousness of Wharton's protagonists, movements of the heart reflect their inner thoughts, and frequent time shifts—particularly the flashback—presage the outcome of these narratives.

Of course, various unusual techniques also distinguish these late tales. In particular, Wharton makes use of her characters' physiognomy to reflect their emotional turmoil: Martha Little's countenance remains "unmoved" when she responds vindictively to her aristocratic relatives' mistreatment; Margaret Ransom's heart beats wildly as she ponders her desire to be rescued from the Wentworth community; and Granice's heart leaps and thumps while he waits to confess the murder he committed ten years ago. Wharton even uses names to echo the entrapment of her protagonists. Margaret Ransom, for example, waits in vain to be "ransomed" from her depressingly dull marriage and the hypercritical Wentworth community. Finally, these later stories abound with references to imprisonment: "prisoner of consciousness," "prisoner at Frostingham," and "the Wentworth tone" all reinforce Wharton's imprisonment theme.

In her early and later tales of prisoners of society, therefore, Wharton presents men and women entrapped by the dictates of society "who find themselves locked into a small closed system, and either destroy themselves by beating their heads against their prison or suffer a living death in resigning themselves to it" (Wilson 198).

Chapter Four

Prisoners of
Art and Morality ⸺⸺⸺⸺⸺⸺⸺

Edith Wharton made several pronouncements concerning morality and the short story. In *The Writing of Fiction*, she points out, "A good subject . . . must contain in itself something that sheds a light on our moral experience" (28). Later, she adds: "There are cases, indeed, when the short story may make use of the moral drama at its culmination. If the incident dealt with be one which a single retrospective flash sufficiently lights up, it is qualified for use as a short story" (*WF* 43). All six stories in this chapter deal with an incident that a "single retrospective flash sufficiently lights up." And all of them involve "a good subject" that "sheds a light on our moral experience." In these tales of art and morality, Wharton's heroes and heroines are creative artists or avid collectors of art who find themselves trapped in a moral dilemma, often of their own making, and become "prisoners of consciousness" when they attempt to resolve it. Once again, to examine the marked development in Wharton's thematic and technical artistry, three of her early tales—"That Good May Come," "The Recovery," and "The Angel at the Grave"—are compared to three from her major and late periods—"The Potboiler," "The Verdict," and "The Daunt Diana."

In her early tales of art and morality, Wharton falls back on familiar techniques. Irony, for example, dominates her character portrayals: her imprisoned protagonists discover that sacrificing themselves "that good may come" leaves them guilt-ridden over their "unprofitable sacrifice" (1: 253). Not surprisingly, the rooms of Wharton's entrapped victims remain significant: Birkton's dilapidated little room in "That Good May Come," Keniston's "bare and shabby" (1: 261) studio in "The Recovery," and Paulina's "forbiddingly cold" (1: 254) library in "The Angel at the Grave" reflect the entrapment each endures.

There are also a number of fresh techniques in these early tales. Wharton makes use of churches, art galleries, and museumlike houses as appropriate settings for her protagonists to suffer their moral dilemmas. Likewise, she exploits creative works of art: Birkton's scandalous squib, Keniston's art exhibition, and Paulina's biography of her grandfather provide "good subjects" that shed "light on our moral experience." Also distinguishing these early tales is the juxtaposition of light and dark to parallel the choice between good and evil facing Wharton's central characters. In "That Good May Come," for example, Wharton contrasts metaphors of innocence and purity—"the snowy crudeness of the outer world" and "the long white procession of choristers" (1: 35)—with images of blackness and shame—Birkton's labeling himself "a damned blackguard" (1: 40) and describing his sister's dress as "black—black as pitch" (1: 39)—to highlight the moral dilemma confronting this poverty-stricken poet.

In her later tales of art and morality, Wharton also employs a number of familiar techniques. Satire is once more combined with irony, and the dialogue remains spirited. A surprise ending also appears in one of the tales, "The Potboiler": "Edith Wharton had a fatal weakness for the anecdote," Blake Nevius tells us, "for the situation capable of taking a surprising turn" (28). Of course, time shifts, particularly the flashback, and the interior monologue are more in evidence: Stanwell's contemplation of the past in "The Potboiler," Gisburn's recollection of the Stroud sketch in "The Verdict," and Neave's reminiscences of the Diana in "The Daunt Diana" help explain why these characters have become prisoners of consciousness.

Wharton's execution of point of view in these later tales also merits attention. She narrates two, "The Verdict" and "The Daunt Diana," from the first-person point of view—about one-quarter of Wharton's tales are recounted by a first-person teller—to enable her reader to come to know "the looks and ways and words of 'real people' " (*BG* 211–12) firsthand.

"That Good May Come" (1894), an uncollected tale from Wharton's early period, recounts the plight of Maurice Birkton, a poor, fledgling poet, who, when faced with the moral dilemma of whether or not to debase his creative talent to benefit another, bows to external pressures and prostitutes himself and his art. Immediately, he realizes the horror of doing evil "that good may come" (1: 39) and is left imprisoned with shame and guilt.

As in Wharton's early "Mrs. Manstey's View" and "Friends," symbolic settings predominate: Birkton's "little room," with its peeling wallpaper, "thirty or forty worn volumes," and "cracked pitcher and basin" (1: 25), mirrors his impoverished existence. The narrative is also framed: conversations between Birkton and his friend, Helfenridge, open and close the tale to create the impression of confinement, of imprisonment. Their exchanges, though a bit tedious at the beginning and melodramatic at the end, reveal the extent of Birkton's guilt-ridden imprisonment. Finally, Wharton juxtaposes light and dark—with repeated references to white and black—to highlight her protagonist's moral dilemma.

The story begins in the shabby bedroom that Birkton, writer of literary criticism and "dreamer of dreams" (1: 21), occupies. He and Helfenridge are bemoaning the rejection of Birkton's latest endeavor, "The Old Odysseus," an epic poem that presents all the great heroes and heroines with "real" human feelings, not just "the obligatory virtues" (1: 21) previously attributed to them. Helfenridge feels that Birkton's unconventional approach to the classics "tallies wonderfully with the inconsequences and surprises that one is always discovering under the superficial fitnesses of life" (1: 21), an observation that foreshadows the surprise ending of the tale. He begins reciting a number of the "fine" verses from his friend's poems, lines filled with images that suggest imprisonment—the "close-locked fingers" (1: 22) of Odysseus and Circe and "Celline in his prison" (1: 23) talking with Christ.

For Birkton understands imprisonment quite well. His desire to earn a living as a poet has certainly restricted his life. Until now, he has received only one offer of a hundred and fifty dollars for an "idiotic squib" (1: 24) about Mrs. Tolquitt, a pretty married woman, and Blason, a man with whom she has been seen alone. Although he originally wrote the witty little piece to amuse a few friends, Birkton is ashamed of its scandalous content. Hence, he promptly rejected the offer. To accept it would mean prostituting himself as a writer.

When his friend departs, Birkton surveys his "ignoble quarters" (1: 25) and compares them to the pleasant home he and his family occupied one year ago before he resigned a warehouse clerkship to pursue a literary career. His present "sordid surroundings"—"the yellowish-brown paper," "discolored plaster," "ink-stained desk," and "rickety washstand of ash" (1: 25)— are grim reminders of his impoverished state. As Nevius points out; "Edith Wharton's imagination could occasionally be roused to symbol-making activity by the conjunction of a theme and a setting" (129). Even a "blurred looking glass" (1: 25) mirrors Birkton's disillusionment. For he has failed as a writer. In fact, his book reviews secure so little money that his mother has had to supplement their income by copying visiting lists for society matrons and writing invitations to society balls.

Particularly disturbing is his mother's revelation that one of the society balls has been canceled, and the "very tidy little sum" (1: 26) she expected to receive will not be forthcoming. Tearfully she informs her son that she does not have the funds necessary to purchase the white muslin dress his fifteen-year-old sister, Annette, is required to wear to her confirmation. She will be the only candidate not dressed in white.

Saddened by his mother's depressing news, Birkton returns to his room, but not before seeing his sister sitting in the kitchen with her arms "flung out across the table" (1: 27). After catching a glimpse of her "red lids and struggling mouth" (1: 27), he retreats to the darkness of his room, "companioned by the dismal brood of his disappointments" (1: 29).

At supper, his misery is exacerbated by his sister's feigned "smooth and serene" (1: 29) demeanor. Although she appears to have masked her disappointment, he cannot forget her earlier tearful face. As the sole support of his mother and sister, he feels he should be able to provide the dress his sister requires for such an important event in her young life.

By one o'clock the next day, Birkton gives Annette $150 to buy a confirmation dress. Once again, as in previous early tales, Wharton provides no penetrating insights into her protagonist's consciousness before he rushed out to sell his scandalous squib. The reader can only conclude that, faced with a moral dilemma—Should he maintain his integrity as a writer, or alleviate his family's distress by selling his scandalous squib?—Birkton placed his sister's need before his own.

Avoiding his mother's query as to which poem he sold, he angrily directs her to take whatever money is left from the purchase of the dress for herself and Annette: "And remember I won't touch a penny of it" (1: 31). He has resolved his moral dilemma, but he is already imprisoned with shame and guilt.

And his guilt intensifies when Helfenridge visits the next evening. Birkton glances at his friend with an "evasive eye" and pushes Annette, dressed "in white muslin, her flat, childish waist defined by a wide white sash, even her little feet shod in immaculate ivory kid" (1: 32), in front of him. But Helfenridge is not so easily distracted. Distressingly aware of what his friend has done, he pointedly asks if he sold the squib. Painfully, Birkton acknowledges his shameful act. He labels himself "a blackguard" and asks Helfenridge, who ignores the question, what he thinks of "a man who's sold his soul" (1: 34).

His distress escalates on Annette's long-awaited confirmation day. As he rides to the church in "a closed carriage" (1: 34)—an image reinforcing

Wharton's imprisonment theme—he glances out the window, hoping to escape his feelings of guilt. But, sadly, his attempt is unsuccessful, and his suffering intensifies as he enters the church. Even the grayish reredos echoes the desolation he feels. At this point in the narrative, Wharton introduces several images of darkness and gloom—the "velvety dusk" and the "raw, sunless daylight" (1: 35)—and contrasts them with metaphors of innocence and purity—the confirmants' "innocent young faces" and "the long white procession of choristers" (1: 35)—to remind her protagonist, symbolically, of his own lost innocence.

Seeing Helfenridge in the back of the church and Annette in the splendid white dress that intimately links her to this "gorgeous sacrifice of praise and prayer" (1: 36), he is somewhat comforted. However, his relief does not last long. His "unquiet eyes" (1: 36) fall on a lady with a young girl dressed in white muslin sitting nearby. His eyeballs burn "like vitriol" (1: 36) as he recognizes the object of his squib and her daughter. Aware that Mrs. Tolquitt's body is shaking with tears, his feelings of guilt return. Her tears seem to choke him. Suddenly suffocated by the smoky incense and fragrant lilies, he rushes out into the white snow where, Wharton tells us, he seems to experience a kind of resurrection, "a new birth" (1: 37). But his deathlike feelings of imprisonment cannot be so easily overcome.

Once home, he shuts himself into his darkened room—Wharton's "intense, continuing interest in enclosures" (Lewis 121) as symbols of imprisonment is patently obvious in this scene—and adamantly refuses to accept the money his mother tells him remains from the confirmation expenses:

> "I don't want the money—I won't touch it. . . . this is Annette's, yours and hers. If you won't spend it for yourself let Annette put it in the savings bank; or let her throw it into the street; I don't care what becomes of it—but don't speak to me of it again. I'm sick to death of hearing about it!" (1: 38)

Emotionally devastated after this outburst, he sits alone until Helfenridge, who had refused an invitation to supper, appears at his door. Immediately Birkton tells him of Mrs. Tolquitt's appearance in church and her impassioned sobbing. After confessing again that his sister's dress was purchased with money earned in the basest and most shameful way, he cries out: "I've done evil that good might come—but it hasn't come—it can't. . . . You think Annette's dress was white? I tell you it was black—black as pitch" (1: 39).

Sobbing uncontrollably, Birkton once again terms himself "a damned blackguard, not fit to look decent people in the face again" (1: 40). Wharton's imprisonment theme dominates the scene as her protagonist stirs uneasily "with the thwarted movements of a caged animal" (1: 40), sinking into "profounder depths of self-accusal" (1: 39). Helfenridge attempts to placate his friend by indicating that good can still come from the act, "that having done evil once it may become impossible to do it again" (1: 40). But Birkton is inconsolable. He encourages Helfenridge to leave so that he can be alone, and once again he sits motionless, inextricably entrapped in agonizing guilt.

As the tale concludes, Helfenridge reenters the bedroom, and, in a further attempt to comfort his downcast friend, informs him that when Mrs. Tolquitt left the church, she was met by Blason, the man in Birkton's squib. He adds that they drove away with the little girl sitting between them. Ironically, Birkton has been castigating himself for writing a scandalous squib that he was convinced, particularly after seeing Mrs. Tolquitt in tears at her daughter's confirmation ceremony, contained no truth. Helfenridge's disclosure about Mrs. Tolquitt, proffered to alleviate his friend's distress, seems to contradict his conviction.

Sean O'Faolain, in *The Short Story*, points out that when a writer concludes a story, "the one thing he must avoid is a sense of bump" (155). Wharton also indicates that "an inadequate or unreal ending diminishes the short tale in value" (*WF* 50). Her ending in this tale fails on both counts: the ending is inadequate, and there is also "a sense of bump." Helfenridge's concluding disclosure about Mrs. Tolquitt, revealed after a conversation with Birkton about good and evil, is presented as an insignificant afterthought rather than a crucial revelation. Furthermore, Wharton's ending the tale without any indication of Birkton's response to Helfenridge's announcement does leave the reader with a sense of bump. Although the fact of Birkton's "one ill act" (1: 40) remains unchanged, there remains unresolved the question of whether his passionate self-deprecation might be somewhat diminished or even ended after his friend's disclosure.

Nonetheless, Lewis, in his biography of Edith Wharton, reports that the editor of *Scribner's* wrote Wharton that "That Good May Come" was "capital" and that he would take "everything else of the same quality you are willing to give me" (70). Although this commendation may be somewhat exaggerated—the narrative has obvious weaknesses—the tale is "capital" insofar as it sheds light on our moral experience. Certainly Wharton's message is clear. In answer to the questions she poses in *The Writing of Fiction*, "What am I being told this story for? What judgment on life does it contain for me?" (27), she responds: Committing a shameful act that good may come leaves the wrongdoer devastated, imprisoned with guilt and remorse.

"The Potboiler" (1904), written during Wharton's major period, describes another impoverished young artist who prostitutes his art in a deluded attempt to help another. Ned Stanwell, the protagonist, sacrifices his artistic convictions to patronize an ailing, financially destitute sculptor and to win the sculptor's sister, whom he loves. Ironically, he is rewarded with rejection. As in many of her early tales, Wharton's setting in this later story is replete with images of enclosure: Stanwell's studio overlooks "a dismal reach of roofs and chimneys, . . . and a December sky with more snow in it lower[s] above them" (1: 663), reflecting the imprisonment her protagonist feels. And as in "That Good May Come," the narrative is framed, with the artist sitting in his dreary studio contemplating his deplorable predicament.

However, distinguishing this later tale is Wharton's skillful use of dialogue. In particular, her use of dialect imbues the tale with both humorous and tragic significance: Stanwell's conversations with Shepson, the crafty picture dealer, both humorously satirize the upper class and tragically spotlight his moral dilemma. Wharton also employs dialogue to spark the surprise ending of the tale: a shocking revelation leaves her protagonist dumbfounded. (However, it does open up the possibility for him to resolve his moral dilemma and free himself from his imprisoned state.)

The tale begins with a description of the shabby quarters of Ned Stanwell, a starving young painter. Immediately the reader discerns that his prisonlike living conditions are not unlike those Birkton endures in "That Good May Come":

> The room was bare and gaunt, with blotched walls and a stained uneven floor. On a divan lay a pile of "properties"—limp draperies, an Algerian scarf, a moth-eaten fan of peacock feathers. The janitor had forgotten to fill the coal scuttle overnight, and the cast-iron stove projected its cold flanks into the room like a black iceberg. (1: 663)

This destitute young artist also refuses to prostitute his artistic ideals by catering to the whims of the wealthy upper class.

A visit by Mr. Shepson, a prosperous picture dealer, only serves to exacerbate Stanwell's misery. Shrewdly, he taunts the young artist about his depressing surroundings, reminding him that he is certainly not as well-fixed as Mr. Mungold, "the fashionable portrait painter of the hour" (1: 663). Stanwell can enjoy the same luxuries as Mungold, Shepson points out, if he would only paint in the same fashionable style. His explanation of "what my gustomers want" (1: 666) provides a perfect opportunity for Wharton to ridicule the artistic taste of the fashion-minded wealthy. Not only does she highlight the societal pressures that in large part have contributed to the imprisonment of her penniless central character, she also decries the wealthy society matrons who want their portraits painted by artists who will give them what they want—"a clever blending of dash and sentimentality, in just the right proportion" (1: 667). She even interjects humor into her satire in her portrayal of Mungold, the prototype of these artists, who paints portraits with backgrounds of gauze and clouds one year and elms and "enormous dogs" (1: 671) the next.

Shepson reports that a wealthy society matron, Mrs. Archer Millington, has seen a portrait Stanwell painted in Mungold's "pseudo-historical style" at the "Fake show," and she wants him to paint her portrait in the same style: "Mrs. Millington don't want a Mungold, because everybody's got a Mungold, but she wants a picture that's in the same sdyle, because dat's de sdyle, and she's afraid of any oder!" (1: 667). However, Stanwell painted his stylish portrait in an "imitative frenzy . . . for the mere joy of the satire" (1: 667); he has no further desire to sacrifice his integrity as an artist just to please a wealthy society matron. Although Shepson has stirred up feelings of envy and resentment in the poor artist, he, like Birkton, initially rejects the monetary offer to preserve his clear conscience.

However, Stanwell is tempted. In a later discussion with his asthmatic neighbor, Caspar Arran, a penniless sculptor who also adamantly upholds "the purity of the artist's aim" (1: 674), he queries: "Why can't a man do two kinds of work—one to please himself and the other to boil the pot?" (1: 671). Stanwell's question serves a twofold purpose for Wharton: it confronts the issue of morality and the artist and presages the moral dilemma Stanwell will soon have to face. Although Wharton believed there is no "water-tight compartment between 'art' and 'morality' " (WF 28), she obviously took a dim view of the artist who painted potboilers.

Arran is appalled by the question, but before he can answer it to Stanwell's satisfaction, he is interrupted by a knock on the door by the "freshly soaped and scented" (1: 671) Mungold. Although Caspar looks on him as "a conscious apostate" (1: 672)—he is "as quick as a dressmaker at catching new ideas, and the style of his pictures change[s] as rapidly as that of the fashion plates" (1: 671)—he nonetheless tolerates Mungold's attention to his sister, Kate, the woman Stanwell also fancies, because of the expensive delicacies he provides.

But Stanwell does not consider Mungold an apostate: he believes that he should be congratulated as "a man whose aptitudes were exactly in line with the taste of the persons he liked to dine with" (1: 673). Even though he has cultivated a deeply personal style and has thus far maintained his integrity as an artist, Stanwell clearly envies the fashionable painter's wealth and affluence. In an extended interior monologue, he acknowledges that Mungold's art is "bad art" (1: 673) but once again questions the artistic ideals that have kept him locked into his impoverished state: "If a man could do several things instead of one, why should he not profit by his multiplicity of gifts? If one had two talents why not serve two masters?" (1: 673).

This moral dilemma is resolved when Stanwell finds himself in a predicament that closely parallels Birkton's in the earlier tale. He learns that Caspar's great work, an allegorical group sculpted in marble, has been rejected for exhibition and that Caspar is deeply depressed. He decides to alleviate Caspar's melancholia—just as Birkton opted to relieve his sister's distress—by repudiating his artistic convictions. He accepts Shepson's offer to paint the portrait of Mrs. Millington for her ballroom and anonymously places an order for Caspar's sculpted group with the money he receives. Like Birkton, Stanwell has prostituted his art in the hope "that good may come."

And initially it seems as though his apostasy will effect the result he desires. Caspar's spirits are certainly raised—in fact, he holds himself up as "the artist who clings doggedly to his ideals" (1: 676). Ironically, he exhorts his colleague to trust in his convictions.

But Stanwell is already an apostate, and, like Birkton, his happiness is short-lived. When Kate and her brother attend an exhibition of the Millington portrait, her "stricken glance" and Caspar's parting shot, "Mungold will have to look to his laurels" (1: 679), remind Stanwell of his "one ill act." Like Birkton, he is imprisoned by feelings of shame and guilt.

Wharton shifts time forward to one year later, and the scene is not unlike that which began the tale. Stanwell surveys the same depressing winter scene that distressed him the year before and acknowledges that the last several months have been miserable for him. Denounced by Caspar and reproached by Kate, he has refrained from painting since spring: "The sight of his tools filled him with a strange repugnance, and he absented himself as much as possible from the studio" (1: 681). Consequently, despite Shepson's revelation that half the wealthy society matrons of the town want him to paint their portrait, Stanwell has delayed accepting their offers. However, he decides he will prostitute his art again if Kate agrees to marry him.

A walk with her in the park in "the double glitter of snow and sunshine" (1: 681) seems to bode well for Stanwell. As she speaks of her brother's ill health and their life together, he seizes what he considers the perfect opportunity to make his plea that she allow him to take care of them both:

"I'm not talking of lending you money; I'm talking of giving you—myself.
. . . Since I painted Mrs. Millington things have changed. I believe I can get
as many orders as I choose—there are two or three people waiting now.
What's the use of it all, if it doesn't bring me a little happiness? And the only
happiness I know is the kind you can give me." (1: 682)

The frozen lake over which they look mirrors the icy refusal that appears
in Kate's eyes. She tells him that her feelings for him have changed since
he painted the Millington portrait. "There's no occasion," she asserts,
"which can justify an artist's sacrificing his convictions!" (1: 684). When
he responds by comparing himself to Mungold, a decent fellow who paints
bad pictures, she argues that Mungold does not realize that his paintings are
"less good than they might be" (1: 683). Stanwell does know, and therein
lies the difference between the two artists. She even announces, shockingly,
that she has promised to marry Mungold, rationalizing that "though his
pictures are bad, he does not prostitute his art" (1: 684). A moment of "high
tension" (*BG* 203), to use Wharton's phrase, follows Kate's revelation.
Stanwell is stunned. His attempt to raise Caspar's spirits and win Kate by
prostituting his art has ended in failure.

In sharp contrast to the brightness of the day when Stanwell began his
walk to the park, dusk has settled when he returns to his dreary studio. He
writes Shepson that he will paint no more fashionable portraits, and, as the
tale concludes, he stares at an unfinished sketch of Kate "with a grim smile"
(1: 684) that bespeaks his recent rejection.

In both "That Good May Come" and "The Potboiler," Wharton introduces an impoverished young artist who initially refuses to sacrifice his
artistic convictions to satisfy popular demand. However, in each tale, the
artist decides to prostitute his art to please a young woman: in the early tale,
to purchase a confirmation dress, and in the later tale, to win her love. Sadly,
in both tales, the artists learn that "good can't come out of evil" (1: 40).

Several techniques—symbolic settings and the use of light and dark, for
example—are also common to both tales and have been noted. More
important, Wharton's use of dialogue in the later tale marks an advance in
her technical achievement. Although both narratives contain conversations
that expose the moral dilemma facing Wharton's protagonists, only in the
later tale do they focus on her protagonist's deliberations over the choice he
must make between equally undesirable alternatives. In "That Good May
Come," the dialogue centers on Birkton's selling his squib and does not
consider the morality of his action until the end of the tale. Only in his final
conversation with Helfenridge does Birkton discuss the question of good
and evil, a question he apparently ignored when resolving his dilemma. In

"The Potboiler," Wharton addresses the immorality of an artist who sacrifices his convictions in Stanwell's first conversation with Caspar Arran. From the beginning of the tale, Stanwell feels morally conflicted by his "heroic devotion to the ideal" (1: 679), and he agonizes over the question repeatedly before arriving at a resolution.

As with the dialogue, the surprising conclusion of the tale also signals a development in Wharton's theme and technique. In the early tale, Helfenridge's unexpected revelation about Mrs. Tolquitt leaves Wharton's protagonist sitting motionless, imprisoned with guilt. In the later tale, Kate's ironic disclosure about her upcoming marriage to Mungold leaves Stanwell in the same position. But he is not motionless. He has returned to his painting. Now that he has been spurned by both Caspar and Kate, who ironically have prospered because of his artistic apostasy, he may be able to free himself from his guilt-ridden consciousness and recover his integrity as an artist.

"The Recovery" (1901), written at the end of Wharton's early period, depicts yet another artist faced with a moral dilemma. But the dilemma in this tale is quite different from those previously discussed. This artist does not agonize over whether to prostitute his art in order to relieve another person's pain and suffering. Instead, he must decide whether to acknowledge his inadequacy as an artist (after he finally realizes what makes a work of art great) or continue painting "bad" pictures.

To enhance her portrayal of an artist imprisoned in a narrow and unimaginative perception of what constitutes art, Wharton exhibits masterful technical skill. In fact, one reviewer of her first short stories points out that this tale was considered "a little masterpiece" (Plante 364). To begin with, Wharton introduces two protagonists: Keniston, the inept, dispassionate artist, who for years views his "bad" (1: 270) paintings "in a musing ecstasy of contemplation" (1: 264), and Claudia, his perceptive, sensitive wife, who from the beginning questions the quality of her husband's work. In truth, both suffer imprisoned lives.

Just as important, Wharton unites irony and satire to advance her comic and tragic purposes: her ironic characterization of the lackluster artist "finishing each picture as though he had dispatched a masterpiece to posterity" (1: 263) and her satiric depictions of the self-proclaimed connoisseurs of art who fawn over his paintings just to be known as those "who collected Kenistons" (1: 260) are indeed humorous. Yet Keniston's awakening to his limitations as an artist and his patron's failure to appreciate his newfound awareness imbue the tale with tragic significance.

Wharton begins her tale with a rather provocative opener: "To the visiting stranger Hillbridge's first question was, 'Have you seen Keniston's things?' " (1: 259). Keniston's "things," the reader is told by an omniscient narrator, are his paintings. The Hillbridge townsmen pose the question because they take special pride in "owning" an artist and all of his best works. They even spread the word "that to 'know' Keniston, one must come to Hillbridge" (1: 259), the inference being that to appreciate fully Keniston's artistry, one must see him in his native milieu. Ironically, only in Hillbridge are his paintings even noticed. One devotee, for example, failed to recognize a Keniston that was exhibited in an art gallery in New York. She remarked, ironically, "It was hiding itself under an incognito" (1: 259), an observation that might also be made about the artist himself.

For Keniston lives a hermitlike existence. He occupies a "bare and shabby" studio in a "small" and "cheerless" (1: 261) house. And although his paintings command a high price, he works "slowly" and "painfully" (1: 261) with frequent periods of inactivity. Consequently, he is not a wealthy man. And, like Stanwell in "The Potboiler," Keniston heroically refrains from painting potboilers. However, unlike Stanwell, Keniston, the omniscient narrator ironically points out, lacks the technical skill required to paint these inferior works of art.

Wharton's explanation of how Keniston achieved his fame as an artist is also delightfully ironic. A professor, reputedly a discriminating collector of art, hung a Keniston sketch in his drawing room. At his instigation—"By the way, have you seen my Keniston?" (1: 259)—his pretentious guests appraised it with "the usual guarded generalities" (1: 259–60), and within two years Keniston's celebrity spread throughout the provincial community of Hillbridge and even beyond. However, the publishers of an elaborate analysis of "the master's methods," obviously aware that his pictures were, in fact, without artistic merit, felt constrained to include a caveat that stated, "Keniston's work would never appeal to any but exceptional natures" (1: 260).

One such "exceptional nature," Claudia Day, is decidedly attracted to Keniston's work, and after reading an article extolling him—it mentioned that he "founded a school, 'created a formula' " (1: 261), and, incredibly, presented three "manners" in his paintings—she travels to Hillbridge, satirically labeled the "fountainhead of knowledge" (1: 260), to see the master and his work. She is somewhat taken aback, therefore, to find a "listless-looking" individual with "a vaguely interrogative gaze" (1: 261). Even more surprising is her discovery that he is poor. And, disappointingly, Claudia also learns that, like his painting, Keniston is "hard to know" (1: 261).

From this point on, Wharton makes repeated references to the word "know" in order to sustain the dramatic irony of the tale. As Margaret B. McDowell points out, Wharton's irony often "inheres in one word that is more serious—or less so—than its context" (*Wharton* 100). Certainly there is little to know about Keniston or his art: indeed, there is little Keniston himself knows about it. He is so imprisoned by his "artistic obtuseness" (1: 265) that he has almost nothing to say about his work. He speaks only when he is interested in something or someone, and since he feels that Claudia says too much that is "cheap, trivial, conventional" (1: 262), he says very little to her during their visit. Consequently, when the visit ends, she hopes they never see each other again.

However, when Wharton begins the next section of the narrative, ten years have elapsed, and Claudia Day has become Mrs. Keniston. Like other early Wharton tales where remarkable transformations take place in the central characters without explanation, the reader is given no insight into the extraordinary reversal that has occurred in the former Miss Day. More important, no clue is furnished to shed light on how this miraculous union came about. The narrator notes only that during her ten years of marriage, Claudia has become distressingly aware that her husband is entrapped in complacency, in a surprisingly "uncritical attitude toward himself and his admirers" (1: 262). Ironically, only she seems to know that his "inarticulateness" regarding his paintings is "not because he mistrust[s] his powers of expression, but because he ha[s] really so little to express" (1: 263). To Claudia's dismay, he seems quite satisfied with his artistic achievement.

Nonetheless, despite her misgivings, Claudia steadfastly avers that she is "the wife of a great artist" (1: 264). After all, his pictures are soon to be exhibited in Paris. The Hillbridge circle also remains enchanted with his works. Incredibly, he continues to attract great numbers of fresh "appreciators" (1: 262). Comic satire enlivens Wharton's depiction of his latest, the "too young, too rich, too inexperienced" (1: 263) Mrs. Davant, "who ordered pictures recklessly, who paid for them regally in advance, and whose gallery was, figuratively speaking, crowded with the artist's unpainted masterpieces" (1: 263). This wealthy socialite is so fascinated with Keniston's artistic creations that she commissions him to paint a series of panels for the Memorial Library. But before he begins, Mrs. Davant suggests, ironically, that he visit Europe—"the home of his ancestors"—in order to "see the work of the *other* great masters" (1: 264). She even advances the money for the panels so that he can afford the trip.

The Kenistons do visit Europe. But before they leave Hillbridge, the artist informs his somewhat surprised wife (who is, in truth, a bit resentful of Mrs. Davant's youth and wealth) that he wishes to "measure" his paintings with those hanging in the museums of Europe. Immediately she interprets his desire as the first acknowledgment of "a sense of possible limitation" (1: 265). She asks if he is sure he can paint the Davant library panels, and Keniston's response, "Immensely sure" (1: 265), rings with his customary self-confidence. He adds only that he feels that painting the panels will freshen him up. This aside reinforces Claudia's suspicion that her husband may be "dissatisfied with his work" (1: 265), and, most important, it foreshadows the conclusion of the tale.

Further indications of Keniston's "sense of possible limitation" occur when they arrive in Europe. They spend a week at the National Gallery in London, where he scrutinizes the paintings on exhibition, carefully noting their similarities and differences. Clearly, he is comparing his work to that of the masters, yet he reveals nothing of his observations to his wife: "He seemed to have a sort of provincial dread of showing himself too much impressed" (1: 266).

In contrast, Claudia has difficulty restraining her feelings. Wharton's graphic description of her protagonist's reaction to the pictures in the National Gallery as she moves from painting to painting and from room to room leaves no room for ambiguity. Claudia is clearly impressed. She observes that "the vast noiseless spaces seemed full of sound," and she "[feels] herself carried off her feet by the rush of incoherent impressions" (1: 266). Struggling not to compare her husband's work with that of the masters—she "knows" she has never experienced such emotion viewing his paintings—she takes refuge "in a passionate exaggeration of her own ignorance and insufficiency" (1: 267).

In Paris, Keniston suggests that he and Claudia go to the Louvre to see the work of "the other chaps" (1: 267). In contrast to the silence that accompanied his trips to the National Gallery in London, Keniston begins to discuss his impressions after just one visit to this Paris museum. Again Claudia wonders if he is beginning to recognize his deficiencies as an artist in order that he might "find his way about in a corner of the great imaginative universe" (1: 267).

Her suspicions are confirmed when Mrs. Davant asks Keniston to discuss his paintings at the exhibit in Paris. Wharton's satire brims with humor as she describes Keniston's admirer remarking that his interpretations are "what ma[ke] them [his pictures] so interesting!" (1: 268). Typically, Keniston demurs, adding, "If my pictures are good for anything they oughtn't to need explaining" (1: 268). He is clearly incapable of complying with her request and chooses instead to remain at home.

Claudia meanwhile walks the Paris streets alone and becomes passionately aware of "an artistic sensibility pervading every form of life" (1: 269).

Hoping this "artistic sensibility" extends to her husband's work as well, she decides, on an impulse, to visit the gallery where his paintings are exhibited. The reader is not surprised that her response to these paintings is quite different from her reaction to the masterpieces hanging in the sound-filled rooms in London's National Gallery. Significantly, Claudia hears no sounds emanating from her husband's paintings. Instead, they strike her

> as odd gaps in the general harmony . . . the miracle, the mirage of life and meaning, had vanished like some atmospheric illusion. . . . She tried to rally her frightened thoughts; to push or coax them into a semblance of resistance; but argument was swept off its feet by the huge rush of a single conviction— the conviction that the pictures were bad. There was no standing up against that: she felt herself submerged. (1: 270)

Crushed by her newfound awareness, Claudia stares at the wall before her as if catatonic. Wharton's word "know" surfaces again as she questions, "How, after all, did she know that the pictures were bad?" (1: 271). Ironically, she struggles to convince herself that she is not qualified to evaluate her husband's art. And, for the moment, she succeeds—that is, until she spots Keniston seated nearby with his head bowed. Instinctively, she knows that he, too, has become aware of the mediocrity of his work.

In truth, Wharton's protagonist has been profoundly affected by all that he has seen. His trips to the National Gallery and the Louvre, where he studied the paintings of the masters in rooms full of "murmur[s] of meaning" (1: 266), have triggered an awakening in the imprisoned artist. He, like Claudia, realizes that the paintings exhibited in a "noiseless" room devoid of the miracle "of life and meaning" at the Parisian art gallery are "bad" (1: 270). Yes, at last, Keniston really does "know." And, consequently, he is faced with a moral dilemma: Should he continue painting as he has in the past or stop and learn how to paint again?

In the final scene of the narrative, the reader learns how he has resolved his dilemma. Simultaneously, Wharton's use of the word "know" loses its ironic thrust. Keniston explains to his wife that initially he did not "know what they [the big fellows] were driving at," but "gradually, by picking up a hint here and there, and piecing them together, I've begun to understand . . . it all came over me in a flash" (1: 273). He is ecstatic that he has made his discovery while there is still time for him to begin again: "My God! Suppose I'd never known! Suppose I'd gone on painting things like that forever!" (1: 273).

As the tale concludes, Keniston informs his wife that he has told Mrs. Davant she will have to wait for her library panels. He has decided to remain

in Paris until he learns "how to paint them" (1: 274). In effect, he has rejected
the pressures his "appreciators" have imposed on him. Of course, in so
doing, he has opted for a different kind of imprisonment, one that requires
he forsake the "thick curtain of his complacency" (1: 272) and "begin all
over again" (1: 273).

Clearly, the problem of the hasty transformation that occurs within
Wharton's protagonists in a number of her early tales, in particular, "The
Lamp of Psyche" and "The Line of Least Resistance," is also evident in this
tale. Although Wharton notes that Keniston visited the National Gallery
several times "to study the paintings in detail, pointing out differences of
technique, analyzing and criticizing" (1: 266), and that he spent time at the
Louvre which "swallowed [him] up" (1: 272), she does not penetrate his
inner consciousness to expose the anguish this uncommunicative artist must
have experienced after his visits to these famous art museums. The reader
is informed only of his decision to remain in Paris in order to forsake his
"exquisite obtuseness" (1: 274). Hence, he remains "hard to know" to the
end.

"The Verdict" (1908), a tale written during Wharton's major phase,
recounts the story of Jack Gisburn, another would-be artist, who years
before was faced with a moral dilemma not unlike Keniston's in "The
Recovery." He, too, became aware of his limitations as an artist and had to
decide whether to continue to paint bad pictures or learn how to paint with
"life and meaning" (1: 270). Unlike Keniston, however, this "fashionable
painter" (1: 660) chose to stop painting completely—he knew he could
never paint like the great masters—and began instead to accumulate "objects of art and luxury" with his wealthy wife's "big balance" (1: 656).

As in the early tale, irony and satire dominate Wharton's portrayal of her
protagonist who, like Keniston, became so imprisoned by the adulation and
artistic demands of well-to-do society matrons that he failed to recognize
his shortcomings as an artist. Significantly, Wharton also introduces several
unusual techniques in this late tale. For one thing, to mirror the two faces
of her protagonist, Wharton makes use of two quite different symbolic
settings. Her description of the luxurious villa on the Riviera with its
"marble Emperors" and "terra-cotta nymphs" (1: 657) exposes the public
side of this former splashy artist, and her sketch of the villa's one "dark plain
room" (1: 659) reveals the private, self-effacing man he has now become.
More important, Wharton frames her tale with a first-person teller. However, because this focus "does not admit of any direct account of mental
process, states of feeling, or motives of persons under observation" (Brooks
and Warren 662), Wharton also makes use of an extended illuminating
flashback that delves into the consciousness of her central character to

explain why, years before, he abdicated his art but still feels imprisoned by his past "false virtuosity" (1: 658).

The tale begins as Rickham, the first-person narrator, visits the Riviera and reminisces about Jack Gisburn, a former artist who lives in a villa nearby. In a brief flashback marked by Wharton's caustic satire, Rickham recalls the time when Gisburn gave up his painting "in the height of his glory" (1: 655). It was an abdication richly deserved, Rickham remarks, for Gisburn was "a cheap genius—though a good fellow" (1: 655) who deserved no glory. Nonetheless, his "purblind public" (1: 660), in particular, his women admirers, deemed him "the man of the moment" (1: 657), a title that contributed in part to Gisburn's faulty perception of himself as an artist. Wharton satirically portrays one of these "interesting women" (1: 656), Miss Hermia Croft, crying over one of Gisburn's mediocre paintings moaning, "We shall not look upon its like again" (1: 655). In sharp contrast, Rickham remarks wryly, Gisburn's colleagues expressed few regrets when he stopped painting and he himself accepted Gisburn's decision "with equanimity" (1: 655).

Now, years later, Rickham is overcome with curiosity. Swiftly, Wharton shifts to the present to recount her narrator's visit to the former artist to discover the reason for his "unaccountable abdication" (1: 655). He knows that Gisburn's wealthy wife is not to blame—he did not marry her until nearly a year after he arrived at his irrevocable decision—but neither did she encourage him to return to his art. Instead, with her enormous riches, she made possible the lavish villa they now enjoy. At this point, Wharton interrupts her narrative to describe the villa's "spacious white-paneled room, with its famille-verte vases," "pale damask curtains," "eighteenth-century pastels in delicate faded frames" (1: 656), and exquisite porcelain and silver in order to reinforce the mental image of opulence she wishes to convey.

But, Rickham points out, Gisburn's wife does not object to her husband's costly acquisitions. In fact, she is delighted with his extravagant purchases, noting that he is "so morbidly sensitive to every form of beauty" (1: 656). Nonetheless, the former artist, who had always thrived on unconditional adulation, now winces at his wife's testimonial. Clearly, he has no desire to be held up "as an object for garlands and incense" (1: 657). He even comments that her accolades should be directed to Victor Grindle, the young artist who has since replaced him as "the man of the moment."

Rickham also observes that none of Gisburn's paintings hangs on the walls. His wife quickly explains that her husband is truly a modest person and that only her portrait remains in the villa—the others have been sent away. She nervously agrees to let him see it "while he's [Gisburn] not looking" (1: 657). As she leads the way past "the marble Emperors of the hall," the "terra-cotta nymphs poised among flowers at each landing," and the *"jardiniere* full of pink azaleas" (1: 657–58), the reader is once again reminded of the "pervading sense of art and literature and culture" (Cooper 170) that distinguishes Wharton's work.

To his surprise, Rickham has difficulty finding the portrait. Eventually he spots it in "the dimmest corner of her boudoir" (1: 657) and observes, ironically, that this humble placement is contrary to Gisburn's former practice. Nonetheless, despite its inconspicuous location, Rickham is still able to detect vestiges of the flash that dominated this former artist's work: "all the hesitations disguised as audacities, the tricks of prestidigitation by which, with such consummate skill, he managed to divert attention from the real business of the picture to some pretty irrelevance of detail" (1: 658).

And he discovers other signs of the same pretentiousness when Gisburn invites him on a tour of the house. Wharton's satire, "a condiment that permeates her entire work with caustic tang" (Russell, "Melodramatic" 432), surfaces as she describes "the bathrooms, the speaking tubes, the dress closets, the trouser presses" on display as "complex simplifications of the millionaire's domestic economy" (1: 658). Although Rickham appropriately compliments his host on the extravagant accoutrements, he admits that he wants to exclaim, "Be dissatisfied with your leisure!" as he had formerly wanted to say, "Be dissatisfied with your work!" (1: 659). (Wharton is, of course, voicing her own sentiments regarding the frivolous preoccupations of the upper class.)

Imagine Rickham's shock, therefore, when he finds that the room Gisburn designates as his own is empty and unadorned. There are "no 'effects' " (1: 659) and no evidence of its ever having been used as a studio. And, significantly, there is no evidence of the expensive furnishings that decorate the rest of the villa. Clearly, in this room, the former artist is stripped of pretension. For the first time, Rickham realizes that Gisburn may no longer be the "cheap genius" he has always considered him. He conjectures that the former artist may be hiding behind his luxurious trappings to escape his painful past. However, he is still somewhat reluctant to accept this newfound insight and asks Gisburn if he ever paints. The emphatic reply, "Never think of it, my dear fellow—any more than if I'd never touched a brush" (1: 659), coupled with the vague expression in his eyes and the added color in his cheeks, leads Rickham to conclude that, in reality, the opposite is true.

But it is not until Rickham spots a Stroud sketch of "an old tired donkey standing in the rain under a wall" (1: 659) that the former artist reveals what the narrator has already guessed: Gisburn remains imprisoned by his desire to paint like the great masters. Rickham poses a series of questions about the sketch and its renowned artist, and Gisburn, in an extended flashback, recounts the incident that awakened him to the realization that he had never really known how to paint and that he would never paint again.

He tells Rickham that after Stroud died, his wife commissioned him to paint a portrait of her husband in order to proclaim his greatness to the public. Although the famous artist died twenty-four hours before Gisburn began to paint the portrait, he could not escape the feeling that the dead man was watching his every move. He became nervous and wielded wild strokes. He even resorted to his customary bravura tricks.

However, like Keniston looking at the paintings of "the big fellows" on the walls of the National Gallery and the Louvre, Gisburn suddenly spotted the picture of the donkey on the wall. In an instant, he realized that in this simple sketch, Stroud had possessed and recreated his subject, something he had never experienced. Following this discovery, he tells Rickham:

> "I couldn't do another stroke. The plain truth was, I didn't know where to put it—*I had never known*. Only, with my sitters and my public, a showy splash of color covered up the fact—I just threw paint into their eyes. . . . Well, paint was the one medium those dead eyes could see through—see straight to the tottering foundations underneath." (1: 662)

Immediately he informed Stroud's widow that he was too overcome with grief to complete the portrait and recommended she contact Grindle, a popular young artist who had just started on the road to fame. In turn, she gave Gisburn the sketch of the donkey, and he never painted again. At first he could not bear to look at it; however, he has since forced himself and declares to Rickham: "it's cured me—cured me" (1: 660).

As the tale concludes, he acknowledges that he became aware of his inferiority as an artist through the work of Grindle. But, unlike Keniston, who arrived at a similar awareness, Gisburn determined that "it *was* too late" (1: 662) to begin again. Sadly, he confesses, "The Strouds stand alone, and happen once—but there's no exterminating our kind of art" (1: 662).

Both "The Recovery" and "The Verdict" describe self-satisfied artists who for years did not "know" what true art is. They became so imprisoned by "the protective adulation of a narrow, unsophisticated public" (Nevius 23) that they painted each picture as though they were "dispatch[ing] a masterpiece to posterity." However, when they become aware—one in the Louvre, the other while painting the portrait of a great artist—that their art is devoid of "life and meaning," they consciously decide to free themselves from "painting things like that forever" (1: 273). But only one believes, perhaps naively, that he can still learn how to paint. The other has determined that it is "too late."

Both tales also share a number of techniques. First of all, Wharton employs irony and satire to explain how her protagonists became so imprisoned in their technical tricks that they lost sight of "the real business of the picture" (1: 658). She also exploits setting in both tales: her graphic description of the National Gallery and Gisburn's Riviera villa help sustain her imprisonment theme.

However, peculiar to "The Verdict" is Wharton's use of first-person narrators. Because she wished to communicate "the effect of intimacy and involvement to the reader" (Macauley and Lanning 109), she begins with the first-person voice of Rickham, who renders a candid account of what he knows about Gisburn, and then shifts to the voice of the artist himself, who reveals the details of the incident that made him realize he had never really known how to paint. This method of narration is in sharp contrast to the omniscient narrator of the early tale, who never penetrates Keniston's consciousness to reveal what this uncommunicative artist thinks is lacking in his work that necessitates his having to learn how to paint again.

Unquestionably, in the later tale, Wharton has portrayed a more mature artist, one with a more realistic view of his artistic talent. That is not to say that his quitting his showy painting has cured him of the desire to paint. On the contrary, it has only brought him to a sharper understanding of his limitations as an artist. Indeed, Wharton's effective first-person narration and extended flashback make clear to the reader that Gisburn remains hopelessly imprisoned in his desire to paint like the great masters who "stand alone, and happen once."

"The Angel at the Grave" (1901), written during Wharton's early period, depicts the fate of Paulina Anson, the devoted granddaughter of the "great" Orestes Anson, who is so locked into preserving the memory of her illustrious grandfather that she sacrifices "all her youth" and "all her dreams" (1: 250)—she even forsakes the man who loves her—to collect the great man's philosophical writings and complete his biography. Indeed, the dusty documents and discolored volumes deserted by the world, yet guarded by this entrapped victim of fate, mirror her self-imposed imprisonment. Most important, irony penetrates the interior monologues of Wharton's central character as she agonizes over her self-imposed sacrifice, and a variety of enclosure images support the imprisonment theme. In particular, the Anson House with its many rooms and impressive furnishings provides thematic definition.

Wharton opens her tale by introducing the most prominent enclosure in the entire narrative—the Anson House, a "place of worship," where adoring disciples of the late Orestes Anson congregate to exchange "ethical enthusiasms" (1: 247). The House—written "with a capital letter" in commemoration of its most distinguished inmate—is located on an "elm-shaded village street" (1: 245), highlighting its enclosed atmosphere. Moreover, Wharton's graphic description of this "cold clean empty meetinghouse" with its "cold spotless thinly-furnished interior," "sparse ornaments," and "shuttered windows," where "the ladies lived on its outskirts, as it were, in cells that left the central fane undisturbed" (1: 245, 247), suggests a prisonlike milieu.

In truth, Paulina Anson, the "solitary inmate" (1: 245) of the Anson House—the word "inmate" underscores the theme of imprisonment—has lived a sheltered existence since early childhood. The offspring of one of the "great" man's three unintellectual daughters, "she had been born," Wharton informs the reader metaphorically, "into a museum, . . . cradled in a glass case with a label" (1: 245). This striking image of enclosure presages Paulina's entire life—the glass case, a sign of her lifelong dedication to her grandfather's work; the label, a symbol of his celebrity.

As a child, however, Paulina does not feel imprisoned in the House. Coming from an uncultured Western community following the death of her mother, she is at once fascinated by its "high-ceilinged rooms, with their paneled walls, their polished mahogany, their portraits of triple-stocked ancestors and of ringleted 'females' in crayon" (1: 247). Excitedly, she absorbs its colorful history. Gifted with "exceptional intelligence" (1: 247), she even begins reading her grandfather's metaphysical works—indeed, she is the only family member who can read them. Although she is too young to comprehend his "mystic vocabulary," she is nonetheless delighted by "his bold flights into the rarified air of the abstract" (1: 248). In short, Paulina experiences only pleasure and excitement as she wallows in her newfound environment.

Even later, when Wharton's protagonist is at last able to garner "crumbs of meaning" (1: 248) from the great man's prose, she does not feel imprisoned in the House. Besieged by historians, critics, and uninformed ladies who wish to borrow, consult, and verify his documents, she glories in the prominence she has achieved as "interpreter of the oracle" (1: 248). She remains unaware that gradually she is becoming entrapped in the House.

It is only when an adventurous New Yorker, Hewlett Winsloe, arrives in town that Paulina begins to grasp the captive hold Orestes Anson and his impressive House have on her. (Wharton occasionally introduces a young man into her narratives to effect in her female protagonist an awakening to her imprisoned state.) Although young Winsloe is initially interested in Dr. Anson and his work—he had heard him lecture several times—he soon becomes smitten with the "kissable" (1: 248) Paulina, and before long, asks her to marry him. However, realizing her obsession with her great ancestor and the House that bears his name, he informs her that once she becomes his wife, he expects to take her to New York to live. He intends to break the chains that bind her to her grandfather and the "monument of ruined civilizations" (1: 247). Hence, he will not live in the House "on any terms" (1: 249).

Paulina is certainly tempted by Winsloe's marriage proposal. But as she ponders his demand that she leave her sheltered environment, she realizes, suddenly, that she is unable to free herself from "the ghosts of dead duties" (1: 249) and the House that holds her prisoner. At this point in the narrative, Wharton employs an unusually subtle image of enclosure to dramatize Paulina's newfound awareness of her imprisoned state. She tells the reader that Paulina feels something barely perceptible emanating "from the walls of the House, from the bare desk, the faded portraits, the dozen yellowing tomes that no hand but hers ever lifted from the shelf" (1: 249) that she deems disapproval of her impending departure. Consequently, she rejects Winsloe and his ultimatum, convinced that as "guardian of the family temple" (1: 247), she can live nowhere else.

Once her protagonist chooses to remain in the House, Wharton introduces a variety of enclosures to symbolize the extent of her imprisonment and her inability to escape. Certainly Paulina's subsequent decision to author a biography of her grandfather intensifies her imprisonment. For years she immerses herself in this project, which she believes will not only preserve her grandfather's ideas but also lend credibility to her already sacrificed life. Accumulating materials with "a blind animal patience," she explores avenues previous biographers had ignored until "it had become more and more difficult to her to leave the House even for a day" (1: 250). In effect, the House becomes her prison, and she its "solitary inmate."

Paulina is a middle-aged spinster when the *Life* is completed. Still very much determined that her ancestor be recognized and acclaimed, she leaves the House—with difficulty—to bring the completed manuscript to the publisher of her grandfather's works. Regretfully, he informs her that Orestes Anson's ideas are antiquated, that there is no commercial value in her "pious undertaking," and that the public has "gone off; taken another train. . . . If they can't get to a place when they want to they go somewhere else" (1: 250).

Appalled by his response, Paulina searches for reasons why a biography of her famous ancestor is not marketable. She becomes buried in "a labyrinth of conjecture" (1: 251)—a dramatic image of enclosure signaling the extent of her entrapment—and decides to put the fruit of her life's labors aside. Like its imprisoned author, the manuscript is locked into the House.

However, time does not diminish Paulina's obsession with her grandfather's life and work. Although she considers traveling, she remains unable to countenance "deserting her post" (1: 252). The reader is not surprised, therefore, when she reverses her earlier decision and proceeds to investigate why the public has "gone off; taken another train." She begins to reread the "great" man's writings to compare his rhetoric to that of writers of the same school. Although years before she had studied his abstract vocabulary "with delight" (1: 247), now she views "his cloudy rhetoric" (1: 252) with dismay. Once again Wharton employs an explicit image of enclosure (as well as the irony for which she is noted) as Paulina concludes that her grandfather's work "lay buried deep among the obsolete tools of thought" (1: 253).

But the most powerful enclosure in the tale appears when Wharton's protagonist painfully examines what has happened to her life during her unremitting years of sacrifice. Like James Joyce's Gabriel in "The Dead," Wharton's Paulina suddenly realizes that

> she had been walled alive into a tomb hung with the effigies of dead ideas. She felt a desperate longing to escape into the outer air, where people toiled and loved, and living sympathies went hand in hand. It was the sense of wasted labor that oppressed her; of two lives consumed in that ruthless process that uses generations of effort to build a single cell. There was a dreary parallel between her grandfather's fruitless toil and her own unprofitable sacrifice. Each in turn had kept vigil by a corpse. (1: 253)

Deeply disturbed by her discovery, Paulina spends the years that follow building "a wall of commonplace between herself and her illusions" (1: 254)—Wharton describes even Paulina's disillusionment with an enclosure image to reveal the depth of her despair—until one day a "fresh-eyed sanguine" (1: 254) visitor arrives to see the House. Again Wharton introduces a young man into the narrative to rouse her protagonist to a renewed awareness of the bond that still exists between her and her famous ancestor. George Corby, like the Paulina of old, is most impressed with the shady elms outside the House and the books and portraits within. Despite its prisonlike atmosphere—the "forbiddingly cold" library, the "inhospitable hearth," the drawn blinds—the House, Corby exclaims, is "a hundred times better than I could have hoped" (1: 254).

To Paulina's surprise, he indicates that he wishes to write an article on her grandfather because he believes him to be "the greatest—the most stupendous—the most phenomenal figure we've got!" (1: 255). He tells her he is looking for Anson's account of the amphioxus—a theory repudiated by the anatomists and zoologists of his day—which, he believes, if uncovered, will prove him a leader in these fields. Bewildered by this young man's hyperbolic proclamations, but excited by his enthusiasm, Paulina hesitatingly unlocks the drawer holding her ancestor's discarded papers and, with trembling hands, turns over the faded documents he desires.

As he devours its dusty discolored pages, young Corby's reaction to the writings of the "Great Man" echoes days past when Paulina felt as he does now: "We must turn out all the papers—letters, journals, memoranda. He must have made notes. He must have left some record of what led up to this. We must leave nothing unexplored . . . do you know you're the granddaughter of a Great Man?" (1: 257).

But Paulina is still not without disbelief. She asks if he is sure of her grandfather and this project, and he, in turn, asks the same of her. In response, she acknowledges that at one time she believed as he does. Now, however, she feels that her unwavering dedication to preserving her grandfather's memory has "ruined" her life: "I gave up everything . . . to keep *him* alive. I sacrificed myself—others—I nursed his glory in my bosom and it died—and left me—left me here alone. . . . Don't make the same mistake!" (1: 257).

Despite her protestations, young Corby will not be deterred. Smiling, he utters words that Paulina has waited years to hear:

> "You're not alone, my dear lady. He's here with you—he's come back to you today. Don't you see what's happened? Don't you see that it's your love that has kept him alive? If you'd abandoned your post for an instant—let things pass into other hands—if your wonderful tenderness hadn't perpetually kept guard—this might have been—must have been—irretrievably lost. . . . And then—then he *would* have been dead!" (1: 257)

Consequently, before he departs, Paulina promises to help him with his research. She realizes that she is still bound to the great Orestes Anson and his work.

As she returns to the empty House with young Corby's commendations still sounding in her ears, she becomes like the Paulina of old. After years of morbid seclusion, she has recovered her "filial passion" (1: 254). In fact, she "look[s] as though youth had touched her on the lips" (1: 258). Perhaps now she will be vindicated for her "blind faith" in her grandfather and his work. The tale ends as she looks out the window at "the elm-shaded street" (1: 258), an enclosure image symbolizing her continuing imprisonment.

"The Daunt Diana" (1910), "a delicate piece of artistry" (Cooper 180) written at the height of Wharton's major phase, recounts the narrative of Humphrey Neave, a dedicated art collector who becomes obsessed with recovering a collection of rare works of art he once owned. He, like Paulina Anson, sacrifices many years of his life and a large part of his inheritance searching for and ultimately recovering his lost beauties.

Unlike in the early tale, Wharton presents a symbolic setting only in the final pages of the narrative when the narrator describes the three shabby, smelly rooms that house the beautiful art treasures that still hold Neave prisoner. Instead, she focuses her attention on her portrayal of her protagonist, "a queer chap . . . so intelligent and so simple" (2: 50–51), and his lifelong quest for the Daunt Diana. She is able to communicate, to use her words, "the effect of the gradual passage of time in such a way that the modifying and maturing of the characters shall seem not an arbitrary sleight-of-hand but the natural result of growth in age and experience" (*WF* 95–96). Indeed, she traces Neave's "growth in age and experience" from his first glance at the Diana to his light-filled face at the tale's end. Equally important is Wharton's deft use of time shifts. She continually shifts from the present to the past and again to the present to convey "the impression of vividness, of *presentness*" (*WF* 48). This impression is also conveyed by a first-person teller. Like "The Verdict," written two years earlier, this point of view "provides a highly dramatic frame . . . a device for suspense" (Brooks and Warren 661–62): not until the final pages of the narrative does Wharton's protagonist reveal why he has devoted so many years of his life to collecting "his scattered treasures" (2: 58).

The tale has a rather provocative opening, not unlike that of "The Recovery." Ringham Finney, the narrator, asks, "What's become of the Daunt Diana? You mean to say you never heard the sequel?" (2: 50), questions he will answer as the narrative unwinds. The first-person teller, therefore, " 'situate[s]' his tale in an opening passage" (*WF* 53) as he sits down with a friend to recount the plight of the Diana, the "queen and goddess" (2: 52) in a collection of treasures originally owned by a brutish Londoner named Daunt.

Immediately Wharton introduces the first flashback to chronicle the background history of Neave, a Harvard graduate, who journeyed to Rome in an effort "to get as far away from it [Mystic, Connecticut, where he originated] as possible" (2: 51). He managed to eke out a living tutoring reluctant youths and escorting well-bred ladies, and with whatever lire he could accumulate, he amassed an assortment of "little nameless odds and ends" (2: 51). Gradually, his reputation grew as a connoisseur of art, and it was not long before the major art dealers consulted him for an evaluation of their treasures.

But Finney digresses, and Wharton nudges her narrator to recount the occasion when Neave first saw the Daunt Diana. The story moves to some fifteen years earlier, when a London art collector named Daunt asked Neave for an opinion on a few of his pieces. Accompanied by Finney, Neave spotted the Diana, a statue of the goddess of the hunt, for the first time. Once again Wharton has selected a subject from classical mythology to under-score her imprisonment theme—in effect, to symbolize her protagonist's obsessive hunt for this magnificent work of art. Neave reacted as though struck by a *coup de foudre*, a thunderbolt. Later, he was able to give the statue "his first free look," a look that said, *"You're mine"* (2: 52). Of course, it was a look that began his lengthy imprisonment.

Finney also recalls his conversation with Neave about the Diana. At this point in the narrative, Wharton interjects a series of lively exchanges between the two friends that reveal the intensity of Neave's desire to acquire this magnificent work of art. "That's my idea of heaven," he declared, "to have a great collection drop into one's hand" (2: 52). He even expressed a desire to bomb Daunt's house so that he could "be in at the looting!" (2: 53). As the narrator points out, "Neave *wanted* what he appreciated—wanted it with his touch and his sight as well as with his brain" (2: 54). In effect, the beauty of the Daunt Diana so penetrated Neave's consciousness that it held him captive for the rest of his life.

Wharton's next time shift occurs as Finney flashes back to a year after Neave's first look at the Diana. In London again, he was amazed to read that Neave had inherited a fortune and had purchased the Daunt collection. Deciding to look up his old friend, he found him so swamped with people begging to see his works of art that he literally imprisoned himself in his luxurious palazzo. Nonetheless, the narrator did manage to penetrate the crowd and was surprised to detect a "vague apathy" (2: 55) in the collector. He even heard Neave say, without enthusiasm, that he "had to buy the lump" (2: 54). Finney reminded him of his previous "idea of heaven" comment and questioned why he now seemed to be suggesting that his purchase was nothing more than an obligation, a duty.

In response, Neave cited the aggravation of moving to such large, formal quarters and the annoyance of the hordes of women clamoring to see his collection. In a moment of insight, the narrator, back in the present, reveals to his listener that he was certain Neave's "lack of warmth" (2: 55) was in no way related to the quality of his collection, but rather to the imprisoning effect its possession had on its owner.

Shifting to the past again, Finney reports that a year later, he was shocked to learn that Neave was selling the entire Daunt collection. Because he was reputed to be the sharpest collector in Europe, everyone surmised that he was selling his works of art because there must be something wrong with them. Hence, many pieces, including the Diana, sold for half their value.

However, within the year, Neave, still imprisoned by his obsession with the Diana, was buying back the collection, piece by piece, at exorbitant prices. Anxious for an explanation, the narrator hunted Neave down until he located him in London. The collector revealed that prior to inheriting his fortune, he was imprisoned by his desire to acquire the beauties and had to struggle to do so. However, soon after he bought the collection from Daunt with his newly acquired fortune, he realized that

> "The transaction was a *marriage de convenance*—there'd been no wooing, no winning. Each of my little old bits—the rubbish I chucked out to make room for Daunt's glories—had its own personal history, the drama of my relation to it, of the discovery, the struggle, the capture, the first divine moment of possession. . . . my *own* things had wooed me as passionately as I wooed them." (2: 57)

Consequently, although he acknowledged that he was ruining himself financially, he was buying "his scattered treasures" (2: 57) back because they remained the most beautiful available. Two years ago, Finney adds, he met Neave in Paris and learned that he had recovered all the important pieces except the Diana: "I wanted her to want me, you see; and she didn't then! Whereas now she's crying to me to come to her" (2: 58).

With his listener still attentive, the narrator recounts the final chapter of the story of the Daunt Diana. He reveals that one month before, he located Neave in a tenement house in Rome. He lives in "three cold rooms," Finney tells his listener, and, though "shrunken" and shabby, he is "more alive" (2: 59) than he was in his luxurious palazzo. Now he does not have to barricade himself from the throngs clamoring to see his collection. His cold, damp, prisonlike rooms, replete with "pauper linen" (2: 59) and neighborhood smells—a setting reinforcing Wharton's imprisonment theme—free him to take pleasure in his beautiful art treasures without interruption. Finney marveled at the sight of this poor man, who had sacrificed his life and fortune acquiring the treasures that were gathered about him on shelves and chairs in all the corners of his dimly lit rooms.

But he gasped when, as he prepared to leave, Neave opened the door to his sparsely furnished bedroom and showed him where he had placed the Daunt Diana: the statue was ensconced in a niche overlooking his bed.

Although he reveals that he has ruined himself financially, he confesses: "I lied to you that day in London—the day I said I didn't care for her. I always cared—always worshiped—always wanted her. But she wasn't mine then, and I knew it, and she knew it . . . and now at last we understand each other" (2: 59–60).

Back in the present, the narrator remarks that while visiting Neave in his dilapidated rooms, he detected an extraordinary light shining on his face. Here Wharton makes use of yet another classical allusion to account for her protagonist's shining face: just as Cynthia, goddess of the moon, loved and kissed the mortal Latmian, Endymion, so, too, Diana loves and bestows a godlike "Latmian kiss" (2: 60) on her worshiper. Though Neave, like Paulina Anson, remains imprisoned with the treasures that have held him captive for so long, "he'd got hold," the narrator reveals, "of the secret we're all after" (2: 60): a "ripe sphere of beauty . . . [his] idea of heaven" (2: 52).

Admittedly, there are striking similarities in the protagonists of "The Angel at the Grave" and "The Daunt Diana." Both are collectors of art— Paulina Anson, of her grandfather's valuable writings, and Humphrey Neave, of his beautiful art treasures. Both must decide whether to "escape into the outer air" (1: 253) or to allow their collections to possess them. Ultimately both resolve their dilemma by sacrificing years of their lives to their "idea of heaven."

Although the protagonists are quite similar, several of the techniques Wharton employs to recount their stories are very different. In particular, in the later tale, she makes lavish use of time shifts to illuminate the past and highlight her theme. And she relies on dialogue to move her story along. In "The Angel at the Grave," the dialogue is minimal: the only conversation that takes place occurs at the conclusion of the narrative between Paulina and Corby and is marred by her dull, repetitive questions regarding her grandfather: "Then you believe in him?" (1: 255) and "Are you—sure of him?" (1: 257). In "The Daunt Diana," Wharton is "very deft in the springing of new items of information, carefully prepared, the timing of curtains, the isolation of significant bits" (Beach 299), to enable the reader to understand the Diana's mesmerizing hold on her imprisoned central character. Neave's unexpected declaration to Finney at the beginning of the tale regarding his desire to acquire a "ripe sphere of beauty" (2: 52) and his passionate confession at the end reveal the origin and extent of his worship of the Diana.

Of course, when "The Angel at the Grave" and "The Daunt Diana" conclude, the sacrificed lives of Wharton's imprisoned collectors seem brighter. The advent of an eager, enthusiastic young man who will revive the study of her grandfather's work leaves Paulina's lips touched with youth, and the acquiring of the Diana produces an extraordinary light on Neave's shining face. However, it is clear that the continuing faithfulness of Neave and Paulina yields a self-imprisoning reward.

The six tales analyzed in his chapter depict artists or art collectors who become "prisoners of consciousness" when they are faced with a moral dilemma. A few individuals, like Stanwell in "The Potboiler," may be able to free themselves from imprisonment, but most, like Birkton in "That Good May Come" and Gisburn in "The Verdict," remain entrapped in a deathlike existence.

In the early tales analyzed in this chapter, Wharton continues to exploit the enclosed space to define character: Birkton's dimly lit "little room" (1: 25), Keniston's "bare and shabby" (1: 261) studio, and Paulina's "forbiddingly cold" (1: 254) library mirror the imprisonment of her protagonists. Other familiar techniques also reappear. Wharton's portrayals of Paulina Anson and Keniston, who both experience a "sense of wasted labor" (1: 253), are laden with her distinctive irony. Satire becomes both humorous and tragic—humorous in her descriptions of the devotees who indiscriminately admire works of art without knowing why, and tragic in her characterizations of the artists whom they admire.

Wharton also introduces several different techniques in these early tales of art and morality. In "That Good May Come," for example, she juxtaposes light and dark to dramatize the moral dilemma her protagonist faces. In this same tale, she includes a surprise ending for its ironic effect: although Wharton cautions against an "unreal ending" (WF 50), she is not averse to providing an unexpected though realistic twist at the conclusion of her narratives.

In her later tales of art and morality, Wharton's distinguishing techniques—irony and satire—emerge more prominently than before. Irony dominates the action in "The Potboiler"—from the introduction of the poor artist at the beginning of the tale to the astonishing revelation at the end—and satire is especially acerbic in "The Verdict" in Wharton's graphic description of her protagonist's opulent villa. Frequent time shifts also mark these late tales, especially in "The Daunt Diana," where interior monologues and flashbacks illuminate the imprisoned consciousness of Wharton's protagonist. Dialogue is more prominent. In these later tales, in sharp contrast to those written earlier, Wharton makes use of crucial conversations that move the story forward with "a greater effect of continuous development" (WF 73).

Unique to these later tales is a technique that has not been previously discussed: Wharton's use of the first-person point of view. Although she employs an omniscient narrator in most of her tales as the most effective vehicle for her ironic and satiric thrusts, in "The Verdict" and "The Daunt

Diana," she frames her tales with a first-person teller. Limited in his observation of the imprisoned central character, this narrator recounts only those happenings that fall within his purview, thus providing "a highly dramatic frame" (Brooks and Warren 661) for Wharton's imprisonment theme.

In her tales of art and morality, therefore, Wharton creates powerful moral dramas. Her protagonists are invariably faced with difficult choices that leave them prisoners of consciousness when they attempt to resolve them. Occasionally liberation results, but most often imprisonment remains, and once again Wharton employs techniques that most effectively depict the agonizing entrapment that exists "within one's own mental state."

Chapter Five

Prisoners of
the Supernatural _____

Edith Wharton, in *The Writing of Fiction*, remarks that "some of the greatest short stories owe their vitality entirely to the dramatic rendering of a situation" (47). In her tales of the supernatural, Wharton strives for that "dramatic rendering" to sustain her reader's attention and "*make* him believe" (*WF* 38) in ghosts. She acknowledges that it is not easy "to write a good ghost story," that "it is not enough to believe in ghosts, or even to have seen one" (*WF* 37). Certain requirements must be observed. "Every phrase should be a sign-post," she tells us, "and never (unless intentionally) a misleading one" (*WF* 37). In this way, and Wharton quotes an unnamed "wise critic" here, "you may ask your reader to believe anything you can *make* him believe" (*WF* 38).

Wharton further contends that once the purveyor of the ghost story gains the reader's confidence, he must "avoid distracting and splintering up his attention" (*WF* 39):

> The least touch of irrelevance, the least chill of inattention, will instantly undo the spell, and it will take as long to weave again as to get Humpty Dumpty back on his wall. . . . Many a would-be tale of horror becomes innocuous through the very multiplication and variety of its horrors. Above all, if they are multiplied they should be cumulative and not dispersed. But the fewer the better: once the preliminary horror posited, it is the harping on the same string—the same nerve—that does the trick. Quiet iteration is far more

racking than diversified assaults; the expected is more frightful than the
unforeseen. (*WF* 38–40)

Consequently, in each of the four tales of the supernatural discussed in this
chapter, Wharton is careful to posit a "preliminary horror"—the thin white-
faced woman in "The Lady's Maid's Bell," the "old man with bent shoulders" (2: 603) in "Mr. Jones," the grey figure in "Afterward," and the sender
of the mysterious letters in "Pomegranate Seed"—and she "harp[s] on the
same string—the same nerve" throughout each narrative to avoid "distracting and splintering up" her reader's attention.

In the Preface to *Ghosts*, her eleventh collection of short stories, Wharton
presents several additional requirements for the ghost story. She tells us that
the ghost story "must depend for its effect solely on what one might call its
thermometrical quality; if it sends a cold shiver down one's spine, it has
done its job and done it well" (2: 878). There is "no fixed rule" (2: 878) for
producing this shiver, Wharton continues, but recognizing that the vivid
imagination and concentrated attention necessary for believing in ghosts "is
rapidly withering" (2: 876), she cautions the writer to tell his tale of the
supernatural "in the most unadorned language" and "be well frightened in
the telling" (2: 878).

To help effect this "thermometrical quality" in her ghost stories, Wharton,
as is her wont, employs symbolic settings, "unadorned" yet dramatically
presented. In particular, images of enclosure—the "locked room" (1: 463)
in "The Lady's Maid's Bell," the "blue parlor" (2: 605) in "Mr. Jones," the
dark library (2: 155) in "Afterward," and the "shabby library" (2: 763) in
"Pomegranate Seed"—figure prominently. At times, Wharton introduces
nature's elements—the snow in "The Lady's Maid's Bell," the cold in "Mr.
Jones," the "thick December dusk" (2: 153) in "Afterward," and the "cold
spring dusk" (2: 782) in "Pomegranate Seed"—to trigger the cold shiver
running down her reader's spine.

Wharton also believes that "ghosts, to make themselves manifest, require
two conditions abhorrent to the modern mind: silence and continuity . . .
where a ghost has once appeared it seems to hanker to appear again; and it
obviously prefers the silent hours" (1: 876–77). Hence, she focuses on the
"still night" (1: 472) in "the Lady's Maid's Bell," the "silent shelter" (2:
599) of the old house in "Mr. Jones," the "sweet still place" (2: 163) in
"Afterward," and the "deep silence" (2: 785) of the library in "Pomegranate
Seed" as appropriate settings for evoking ghostly visitants.

Not surprisingly, the focus remains on imprisonment in Wharton's tales
of the supernatural. However, unlike in the previous stories analyzed in this
study, the central characters are not imprisoned by love and marriage, by

society's conventions, or by their artistic ideals. Instead, the men and women in Wharton's ghost stories are imprisoned by fear. They are "well frightened" of their enclosed spaces, of the dark and silent night, of the specters that sometimes appear in these eerie settings, and, most important, of their own painful inadequacies, their own ghosts. As Annette Zilversmit points out:

> The final presence of the supernatural only confirms the entrapment of these women in their own long-denied fears. . . . In relegating defeat to forces outside themselves, such women try to avoid pain and responsibility, and keep themselves forever from controlling their destinies. Ghosts are the final confession of one's self-pitying helplessness. (298–99)

In "The Lady's Maid's Bell," for example, Alice Hartley fears her "weak and tottery" (1: 457) condition and her inability to communicate openly. In "Mr. Jones," Lady Jane Lynke, a self-avowed "active, independent" (2: 595) woman, is awestruck in the presence of Bells, her mysterious old ancestral home, and its invisible caretaker, Mr. Jones. Mary Boyne in "Afterward" and Charlotte Ashby in "Pomegranate Seed" are also rendered powerless in their attempts to confront the "inexplicable, intolerable" (2: 767) specter that is destroying their faltering relationships with their husbands—Mary in knowing so little "of the material foundation on which her happiness was built" (2: 161), Charlotte in failing to question her husband's "mysterious letters" (2: 766).

To help free these women from their fear-filled imprisonment, Wharton conjures up supernatural visitants that bring them face-to-face with their dreaded ghosts. Of course, waves of overpowering fear immobilize them each time the ghost appears. As soon as the specter vanishes, however, the fear diminishes, and a period of emotional release follows. These alternating periods of terror and tranquility (which I have labeled "peristaltic") continue until a tragedy occurs, and an "inescapable symbolic truth" (McDowell, "Ghost Stories" 135) is revealed. In a few tales, this truth empowers Wharton's protagonists to escape the prison of their fearsome ghosts.

Wharton wrote only one of her eleven ghost stories during her early period, "The Lady's Maid's Bell"; and as has been the practice in this study, this story is coupled with a tale from her late period containing a similar story line and theme, "Mr. Jones." "Afterward," written during her major phase, and "Pomegranate Seed," appearing twenty-one years later, also share a parallel plot and theme. Both pairings further illustrate the development of Wharton's techniques when presenting the imprisonment theme.

"The Lady's Maid's Bell" (1902), Wharton's first ghost story, recounts the tale of a lady's maid who discovers that her predecessor is appearing from the dead to protect her emotionally fragile former mistress from her sexually abusive husband and to shield her intimate relationship with a handsome neighbor. To accommodate the dark, silent atmosphere she deems necessary for a ghost to manifest itself, Wharton creates a symbolic setting—a dark, isolated mansion and a dreary, overcast milieu. She also furnishes a preliminary horror—the white-faced silent woman dressed in a dark gown—and conspicuous sign-posts—Mr. Brympton's "red face" and Mrs. Blinder's hurried and "trembling-like" (1: 461) speech. Most important, she introduces a kind of peristaltic action—periods of intense fear followed by intervals of untroubled calm—and a first-person narrator to produce a "thermometrical quality" for her ghostly tale.

The tale opens as Alice Hartley, a "quiet, well-mannered, and educated" (1: 458) young woman, learns of a situation as lady's maid and companion to Mrs. Brympton, a "nervous, vaporish" (1: 457) semi-invalid, whose husband is rarely at home and whose two young children have tragically died. Even though she has been warned that the house is dark and dreary and the master lecherous—"you've only to keep out of his way" (1: 458)—Wharton's frail protagonist accepts the position because she has just been released from a three-month hospital stay with typhoid and is low on funds.

Significantly, it is a "dull October day, with rain hanging close overhead" and the daylight "almost gone" (1: 458) when the newly hired lady's maid steps off the train into the dogcart waiting to escort her to the Brympton estate. Paralleling the weather is the Brympton mansion. Situated in the midst of a mile or two of woods and fronted by a "gravel court shut in with thickets of tall black-looking shrubs" with "no lights in the windows" (1: 458), the house is indeed dark and gloomy. Ironically, Wharton's unsuspecting protagonist is not dismayed by this ominous setting. She is, in fact, rather pleased with "the look of everything" and concludes that she will be working in "the right kind of house" (1: 458).

Inside the house, however, she is not so certain. A series of strange happenings make her very uneasy. As she is led to her room, she spots "a thin woman with a white face, and a dark gown and apron" (1: 458–59) who stands silently in the passageway. Surprisingly, no one but Hartley seems to see her. She discovers that the room opposite hers, a room described as "nobody's," is kept locked and that the housemaid becomes "crosslike" (1: 459) when she finds that the door to this mysterious room has been left unlocked. From this point on, Wharton makes repeated references to the woman with the white face and the room with the locked door—the preliminary horrors of the tale, to use her phrase—to evoke fear and, of course, to provide suspense.

When Hartley first meets with Mrs. Brympton, she becomes more apprehensive. She learns that her "delicate-looking" (1: 459) and pleasant-voiced mistress will not ring when she desires her assistance. Although a "special" (1: 460) bell rings from Mrs. Brympton's room to hers, a mystified Hartley is informed that her mistress will ring for the housemaid, who in turn will fetch her whenever she is needed. The novice lady's maid is understandably perplexed.

Added to this puzzlement are the sinister responses of the household help to Hartley's inquiries about the silent, white-faced woman. She is told that no such woman exists. When she expresses a desire to use the mysterious locked room as a sewing room, the cook, Mrs. Blinder—whose name matches her cryptic responses—suddenly becomes white-faced—one of Wharton's revealing "sign-posts"—and warns her, "trembling-like" (1: 461), not to make such a request. The room was Emma Saxon's, Mrs. Brympton's maid of twenty years, and it has been kept locked since her death six months before. Emma worshiped her mistress, Mrs. Blinder reveals, and "my mistress loved her like a sister" (1: 461).

When Hartley meets her master, a man who drinks to excess, curses, and never stays home more than a day or two, she experiences even more discomfort. Wharton's description of this "big fair bull-necked man, with a red face and little bad-tempered blue eyes" (1: 461), foreshadows the end of the tale, when both his bullish behavior and his bad temper are prominently displayed. Hartley also notes her master's salacious glances. Although she is satisfied that she is not "the kind of morsel he [is] after" (1: 461), she is still uneasy whenever he is near. His wife is even more distressed in his presence: she becomes white-faced and cold to the touch.

Only when a neighbor, Mr. Ranford, "a slight tall gentleman of about thirty" (1: 462), arrives for one of his lengthy visits do her color and warmth return. They discuss books, and often he reads to her by the hour. Hartley likes Ranford—he always has a kind word for her and the other servants— but she questions his seemingly cordial friendship with her master. They are so different. She soon discovers that her master finds Ranford's visits irritating, and he often taunts his wife about their neighbor's frequent presence. These unpleasant exchanges between husband and wife disturb Hartley. She concludes that theirs is an "unhappy match" (1: 462).

At this point in the narrative, the strange happenings cease—Hartley's fright subsides, and a period of calm ensues. Nonetheless, she is "never quite easy in [her] mind" (1: 463) each time she reenters the mansion. The room opposite hers continues to frighten her. On rainy nights she imagines noises coming from behind the locked door.

One night her imaginings become a reality. Following a quarrel between the master and his wife regarding the frequency of Mr. Ranford's visits, a jittery Hartley is awakened by the jangling of the lady's maid's bell. She hears the door of the locked room opening and closing and footsteps—a woman's—running down the hall to Mrs. Brympton's room. Paralyzed with fear, she confesses, "I turned cold with the thought of it, and for a minute or two I dursn't breathe or move" (1: 465). She gradually regains her composure, however, and starts to follow "that other woman" (1: 465). Hastening down the long, silent passageway, she sees and hears nothing: "all was dark and quiet as the grave" (1: 465). Wharton has created the perfect setting for a ghost to appear.

By the time the solicitous lady's maid arrives at her mistress's door, she is again overcome with fear. Nonetheless, she is able to garner enough courage to knock repeatedly at the door until her furious master, his savage red face glowering (Hartley intuits that he has been drinking), responds queerly: "*You? . . . How many of you are there, in God's name?*" (1: 466). She becomes even more unnerved when the very weak and faint-voiced Mrs. Brympton unthinkingly calls her *Emma* (1: 466) before sending her back to her room. In this passage, Wharton exposes the master as an abusive man and his wife as an imprisoned victim. And the ghost of Emma Saxon emerges as the protector of her former mistress. As Barbara A. White points out: "The ghosts in Wharton's middle stories are basically protective. They either challenge the villain directly or try to warn the observer or protagonist of impending danger" (69).

However, Wharton's protagonist is too frightened to appreciate what has occurred. She knows that her mistress did not ring the bell—she was too weak for that—but she does not know who did. She also knows that the master was furious with her intrusion. And she can only guess why. Furthermore, she is confused by his query, "*How many of you are there, in God's name?*," and puzzled by Mrs. Brympton's calling her *Emma*.

Nonetheless, the next day Hartley's fear subsides, and she is once again in control. When her master, with his characteristic "angry red spot coming out on his forehead" (1: 467), questions her about an early morning excursion—a "pale and drawn-looking" (1: 466) Mrs. Brympton had sent her to the village with a prescription and a note for Mr. Ranford—the lady's maid, with unwonted boldness, lies rather than divulge the purpose of her errand. She fears there may be something more than friendship between her mistress and Ranford—the note may have been a warning for him to stay away—and she does not wish to betray her mistress to her husband.

But her courage fades when later the same day she learns the identity of the white-faced woman who appeared in the passage on the day she arrived. Because Wharton believed that in a ghost story "the expected is more frightful than the unforeseen" (*WF* 40), she now establishes a connection between the woman and Emma Saxon. While sewing at the broken-down machine in the locked room, Hartley finds a photograph of the mystery woman, whom Mrs. Blinder identifies as the former lady's maid. (This revelation is "expected"; the reader is not surprised that the woman is the ghost of Emma Saxon.)

Of course, Wharton's protagonist is terrified. She becomes "cold all over," and her heart begins "thumping in the top of [her] head" (1: 468). And, not surprisingly, visions of the white-faced ghost of Emma Saxon begin to haunt her imagination:

> Night after night I used to lie awake, listening for it to ring again, and for the door of the locked room to open stealthily. . . . I felt that *someone* was cowering there, behind the locked door, watching and listening as I watched and listened, and I could almost have cried out, "Whoever you are, come out and let me see you face to face, but don't lurk there and spy on me in the darkness!" (1: 469)

She is able to quell her fear, however, when Mr. Brympton departs for a cruise to the West Indies (perhaps she has guessed that the ghost appears only to protect her mistress from her husband's abusive treatment), and Mr. Ranford's visits resume. Within a short time, she finds that she can even walk by the locked room without trembling. Wharton has intentionally interjected a deathlike calm in the narrative before evoking the ghost once more.

The lull is short-lived, however. One wintry day, as Hartley sits admiring the snow—nature's contribution to the cold shiver Wharton hopes to effect in her reader—the ghost of Emma Saxon appears at her door. At first she "couldn't stir" (1: 470). But the ghost inspires her with newfound confidence, and she is able to ignore her fear—for the moment at least—and follow: "This time I wasn't afraid to follow—I felt that I must know what she wanted" (1: 470).

Not even nature's cold deters her. Wharton's powerful description of the lady's maid's trek through the snowy woods with her snow-clad feet "frozen to the ground" and her heart "beating fit to strangle" (1: 471) underscores her ability "to assimilate the very landscape into her art, to make of natural setting as it were an active agent in the unfolding psychic drama" (McDowell, "Ghost Stories" 138). The ghostly figure leads Hartley to Ranford's house. Before she can discover the "dreadful thing" (1: 471) that will befall her mistress, however, Ranford greets her, and the ghost vanishes. Emotionally drained, she passes out, once more overcome by the same "sense of helplessness" (1: 471) she has experienced before.

Another brief period of calm follows, and again Hartley's fear subsides. But not for long. That night she hears the door to the gardens open and close, followed by "the furious ringing" (1: 472) of her bell. Faithful to her conviction that the horrors in a ghost story should be "cumulative and not dispersed" (*WF* 39), Wharton has resurrected the white-faced ghost of Emma Saxon. Peering out her door, Hartley sees the specter, and, as before, she confesses, "For a second I couldn't stir" (1: 472). However, the mysterious sound of a key turning in the house door and the suspicion that the master of the house has unexpectedly returned from his journey to the West Indies enables her to ignore her fear and rush boldly to her mistress's room.

Just as she informs an alarmed Mrs. Brympton of the possibility of her husband's return, he appears at the door and announces that he is "going to meet a friend" (1: 473). With the distinctive "angry red spot" reappearing on his forehead, he pushes Hartley aside and heads straight for his wife's dressing room, where he is confronted by the ghost of Emma Saxon shielding his hated rival, Ranford. But the ghost cannot save the imprisoned Mrs. Brympton. Unable to deal with the shock of her husband's finding her in such a compromising situation, she loses consciousness and subsequently dies.

At the funeral service, Hartley notes that Mr. Ranford is leaning on a stick—possibly as a result of his hasty departure from the Brymptons' bedroom. Brympton stares angrily at Ranford's hobbling gait, and his characteristic red spot pops out "sharp on his forehead" (1: 474) for the last time. Both sign-posts disappear as the tale concludes. The ghost of Emma Saxon has also vanished. Her mistress no longer needs her protection. Most important, her successor has also proved herself a loyal and trusted servant. The courage she displayed defending her mistress has freed her from the ghostly prison of her painful inadequacies.

"Mr. Jones" (1928), a tale written at the height of Wharton's late period, is "a story of indescribable cruelty, imprisonment, and violence set in the 1820s" (Lewis 522). This narrative recounts the tale of another servant, this time a manservant, who appears from the dead to protect his long-departed master from being exposed as the ignoble blackguard that he once was. The protagonist, Lady Jane Lynke, discovers, much like Hartley in "The Lady's Maid's Bell," that Lord Thudeney, like Mr. Brympton, was a womanizer who imprisoned and maltreated his powerless wife.

Likewise, Bells, the portentous English country estate in "Mr. Jones," brings to mind the Brympton country estate in the early tale. Even the memorable portraits, "paneled dining room" (2: 603), "crooked passages" (2: 598), and locked muniment room in Bells recall the "dark paneling," "old portraits" (1: 458), dark passages, and locked sewing room of Brympton Place. Wharton also posits a "preliminary horror"—an "old man with bent shoulders" (2: 603)—and a prominent sign-post—the "odd pallor" (2: 609) enveloping the housekeeper's rosy cheeks—to effect the "thermometrical quality" she desires in her ghost stories.

It is a "lustrous motionless" (2: 594) day in September when Wharton's central character, the "active, independent" (2: 595) Lady Jane Lynke, arrives at Bells, the beautiful old country estate she has inherited from a distant relative. Wharton's description of the padlocked portals, the moat, and the "holly hedges as solid as walls" (2: 595) evokes a fortress. With her remarkable "visualizing power" (Nevius 44) and her extraordinary ability to accommodate setting to theme, Wharton has created an atmosphere of confinement, of captivity, to reinforce her imprisonment theme. Even the "low deep-buttressed chapel" (2: 595) adjoining the house suggests a prisonlike milieu.

Significantly, Lady Jane's imprisonment with fear begins in this chapel. Among the commemorative monuments she spots a bust of the distinguished fifteenth Viscount Thudeney of Bells. Inscribed below his lengthy history, his honors, and his titles is the phrase "Also His Wife" (2: 595). No explanation follows, and Lady Jane is understandably baffled by the strange inscription.

Even more puzzling is Lady Jane's reception at her new home. A "youngish, unhealthy, respectable and frightened" (2: 596) woman hesitantly unlocks the door and then denies her entrance to the house (the half-a-crown bribe Lady Jane offers does not help) with the cryptic pronouncement: "Mr. Jones says that no one is allowed to visit the house" (2: 597). Despite having always prided herself on her "single-handed" prowess when entering the "most closely guarded doors" (2: 596), Lady Jane is intimidated by this inhospitable greeting. And her fear returns that evening when her novelist friend, Edward Stramer, reveals that some thirty years before he, too, was refused admittance to Bells with the same hostile response.

The prisonlike atmosphere within the house also adds to Lady Jane's uneasiness. When she investigates the one-story Bells, with its "low attics," "crooked passages and superfluous stairs" (2: 598), and "narrow walled-in staircase" (2: 614), she makes the insightful observation that in its lengthy history, the old house was probably looked upon as a "cradle, nursery, home, and sometimes, no doubt, a prison" (2: 599). Gary Lindberg asserts that

Wharton's metaphors "clarify immediate issues" (158), and the introduction of the metaphor of house as prison at the beginning of the tale foreshadows Lady Jane's subsequent discovery that in the past the house was indeed a prison.

The prison metaphor is also evident in the costume of Mrs. Clemm, the strange housekeeper of Bells. Wearing a funereal "black silk" bodice and skirt, "a black lace cap," and "a heavy watch chain" (2: 599), morbid garb symbolic of her prisonlike existence with the invisible Mr. Jones, she appears the perfect jailer. Her eyes are also black, "like black seeds" (2: 599), Wharton tells us, mirroring the absence of life. Even her rosy cheeks camouflage an "odd pallor" (2: 609) that surfaces whenever Lady Jane asks to see "the guardian of Bells" (1: 602). Significantly, Mrs. Clemm's rosy cheeks glow when she is successful at concealing information about Mr. Jones and pale whenever she fears that Mr. Jones's whereabouts may be revealed. Like Mrs. Blinder, the cook in "The Lady's Maid's Bell," Mrs. Clemm also responds to probing questions about Mr. Jones (whom she identifies as her great-uncle) indirectly or not at all. When Lady Jane asks who Mr. Jones is, Mrs. Clemm, her cheeks paling, enigmatically replies that he cannot be seen because he is presently "more dead than living" (2: 600). And when Lady Jane asks to be taken to Mr. Jones, the discomfited housekeeper responds that "he's between life and death, as it were" (2: 601). Just as Hartley is unable to secure information about the ghost of Emma Saxon, so, too, Lady Jane is rebuffed whenever she inquires about the elusive Mr. Jones.

A few days later, she shares Mrs. Clemm's cryptic remarks about the yet-to-be seen Mr. Jones with a group of friends from Kent. Even a warning regarding the inutility of the blue parlor with the citron wood desk is laughingly passed along. It is not until one of the ladies leaves her handbag in the blue room and Lady Jane goes to retrieve it that her fear returns. She is certain that she sees "an old man with bent shoulders" (2: 603) at the desk. However, a closer look reveals that no one is there: only the needlework curtain stirs slightly. From this point on, Wharton harps on the old man with bent shoulders in much the same way that she harps on the white-faced woman behind the locked door in "The Lady's Maid's Bell." Just as Hartley cannot pass the locked door "without a shiver" (1: 467), Lady Jane "shiver[s] a little" (2: 604) whenever she thinks about the man in the blue parlor.

When Stramer returns for a few days, Lady Jane's confidence is restored. Acting as the perfect hostess, she even requests that a fire be lit in the blue parlor. However, Mrs. Clemm continues to object to the use of the parlor: Mr. Jones has ruled that "the chimney in the blue parlor isn't safe" (1: 605).

Her courage fading quickly, Lady Jane defers to the still invisible Mr. Jones—just as she did at the beginning of the tale when her feelings of inadequacy first surfaced—and she and Stramer retreat to the salon.

Focusing their attention on a portrait of Lady Thudeney, the woman to whom the inscription on the chapel monument refers, they note that the portrait was painted in the blue room near the citron wood desk and that the woman in it "looked out dumbly, inexpressively, in a stare of frozen beauty" (2: 606). At this point in the narrative, Wharton interjects a spirited conversation between the two friends heavy with imprisonment images. Stramer suggests that they visit the archives to learn more about the "strange face" (2: 606); however, Lady Jane informs him that the key to the muniment room has been mysteriously lost. She adds, ironically, that the locksmith Mrs. Clemm summoned has mysteriously died. To this rather shocking revelation, Stramer sarcastically replies, "Well, in Mrs. Clemm's hands keys get lost, chimneys smoke, locksmiths die" (2: 607).

But he will not be deterred from his search for the mysterious Mr. Jones. He insists that they visit the blue parlor to see "what's happening now" (2: 607). Lady Jane laughingly acquiesces, but in the doorway her heart jerks with fear as she urges Stramer away from the citron wood desk. (Throughout this late narrative, Wharton makes use of heart and hand imagery to signal her protagonist's recurring bouts with fear.) She becomes more frightened when she thinks she sees the needlework curtains stirring again. And her fear does not subside.

The peristaltic action of the tale builds as Wharton introduces a series of suspenseful happenings. Lady Jane finally visits the muniment room but not before delivering a threat to Mrs. Clemm that she will break the lock or even the door to the room if necessary. Not surprisingly, Mrs. Clemm, her face "bathed in that odd pallor" (2: 609), produces the lost key. However, the papers with information on Lady Thudeney are missing. Fresh footprints on the dusty floor suggest that someone has recently visited this deserted room and perhaps removed the incriminating papers. Lady Jane suddenly feels "a chill of a different and more inward quality," which intensifies when Stramer determines that the prints belong to a man, "an old man with a shaky uncertain step" (2: 610). Lady Jane opines that Mr. Jones has removed the missing papers, but she is too frightened to pursue this avenue of thought: "I'm freezing, you know; let's give this up for the present" (2: 610).

But when she spots the same strange dusty footprints heading for the blue parlor, she can no longer dismiss her fear. Significantly, she feels the "same inward shiver" (2: 610–11) she experienced the first time she encountered the old man in the blue parlor. As she pushes the door open, she is certain that she sees an old man sitting at the citron wood desk. However, Mrs.

Clemm calls to her, and when she looks back, only the faint movement of the curtain remains.

Now visibly trembling with fear, but with determination not unlike Hartley's when she fearlessly follows the ghost at the conclusion of "The Lady's Maid's Bell," Lady Jane courageously heads for the desk. Paling—Wharton's penchant for describing facial coloration is evident throughout this late tale—Mrs. Clemm warns her mistress not to open the desk drawers where Mr. Jones's private papers are kept. Just as Mr. Brympton throws up his hands to shield his face from Emma Saxon's ghost in "The Lady's Maid's Bell," Mrs. Clemm, upon hearing Lady Jane's declaration that she has seen Mr. Jones and intends to survey his papers, raises her arms "as if to fend off a blaze of intolerable light, or some forbidden sight" (2: 611).

Nonetheless, despite her bold announcement, Lady Jane opens the desk with a "slightly shaking" (2: 612) hand—more physical evidence of her fear-filled state—and finds the missing papers. Among them is a letter from Lady Thudeney to her husband, deploring

> that close seclusion in which Mr. Jones persists—and by your express orders, so he declares—in confining me. . . . to sit in this great house alone, day after day, month after month, deprived of your company, and debarred also from any intercourse but that of the servants you have chosen to put about me, is a fate more cruel than I deserve and more painful than I can bear. (2: 612–13)

Like Mrs. Brympton, this wealthy deaf and dumb woman had been manipulated into marriage by a philandering husband and then imprisoned in a mansion while he reveled abroad, gambling and womanizing.

Jane shivers again as she ponders this woman's imprisonment and Stramer's suggestion that Lady Thudeney's jailer and Mrs. Clemm's Mr. Jones may be one and the same. Before she is able to respond to this terrifying possibility, "a livid, dishevelled" (2: 614) Georgiana, the same frightened young woman who denied Lady Jane entrance to Bells at the beginning of the tale, announces that Mrs. Clemm will not respond to her, that she seems dead.

Rushing to the housekeeper's room, they are horrified to discover that she has been strangled. Removed from Mr. Jones's control, she has become "someone else": the "red-apple glaze" is gone from her cheeks, and her eyes manifest an "unspeakable horror" (2: 615).

Lady Jane's shivers recur when she asks Georgiana the whereabouts of Mr. Jones and is told that he has been dead for years:

"He's in his grave in the churchyard—these years and years he is. Long before ever I was born . . . my aunt hadn't ever seen him herself, not since she was a tiny child. . . . That's the terror of it . . . that's why she always had to do what he told her to . . . because you couldn't ever answer him back. . . . " (2: 616; Wharton's ellipsis)

Her response overflows with ellipses—a technique Wharton employs lavishly in her later tales to signal the extent of her characters' distress. Even from the grave he continued to rule Mrs. Clemm, Georgiana adds, and her death is clearly punishment for allowing Lord Thudeney's secret papers to be revealed: "You hadn't ought to have meddled with his [Mr. Jones's] papers, my lady. . . . That's what he's punished her for" (2: 616). But Wharton's protagonist need no longer fear. She has confronted her ghost—the mysterious Mr. Jones—and he no longer "still rules" (2: 605).

Clearly, "The Lady's Maid's Bell" and "Mr. Jones" are tales of victimization and imprisonment. In both tales, Wharton portrays a wife who has been imprisoned by a philandering husband, a ghost who protects a former employer's honor, and a central character who is fearful of her own ghosts. Remarkably, in the early tale, the ghost of Emma Saxon imbues Hartley with confidence, and she is no longer afraid of her newly acquired position and her ghostly predecessor. In "Mr. Jones," the final appearance of the "old man with bent shoulders" and the discovery of Lady Thudeney's abusive husband also inspire Lady Jane to conquer her ghosts—her awesome ancestral home and its mysterious ghostly past. Both women, therefore, are no longer imprisoned by a paralyzing fear of their own painful inadequacies.

Wharton also observes her requirements for "a good ghost story." She posits a preliminary horror and memorable sign-posts and initiates a kind of peristaltic action to provide a thermometrical quality for her tales. However, there is a richer supply of dialogue in the later tale. In "The Lady's Maid's Bell," the conversations are minimal—there are only a few occasions when Hartley talks with the other servants and fewer yet when she speaks to her employers—and these exchanges reveal little of significance. In "Mr. Jones," dialogue fills almost every page. The shocking revelations about Mr. Jones and his master are divulged in Lady Jane's conversations, particularly those with Mrs. Clemm, and many of their painful exchanges alert the reader to the paralyzing fear imprisoning Wharton's central character.

Furthermore, a remarkable change occurs in the configuration of the ghost. In "The Lady's Maid's Bell," the ghost appears not as a disembodied spirit but as a woman who can be seen. The reader knows who she is from the beginning. In "Mr. Jones," the ghost appears only as a faint shadow—he is never well defined. This difference in form is obviously a suspense-geting device: the reader is curious to learn the reasons for Mr. Jones's mysterious appearances at the citron wood desk. However, Wharton still fails to effect the cold shiver in the reader that she desires—the element of suspense is wanting in both tales. Nonetheless, she does fashion absorbing narratives that faithfully record the onset and overpowering nature of fear.

"Afterward" (1910), written during Wharton's major period, recounts the story of Ned and Mary Boyne, an American couple who come to England from the Midwest to engage solely in "harmonious activities" (2: 154). Sadly, their idyllic existence is disrupted when the ghost of a man Ned bilked out of a fortune comes to their country home and spirits Ned away with him.

Before beginning a discussion of this tale, it should be noted that there is some difference of opinion regarding its artistic merit. Lewis contends that it "begins promisingly but wilts into melodrama" (296). In contrast, Douglas Robillard maintains that

> the remarkable substantiality of the story comes from the careful and full
> characterization of Mary Boyne, the perfectly ordinary surroundings in
> which the ghostly events take place, the fact that they happen during the
> daytime, and the decidedly commonplace appearance of the ghost as a quiet,
> polite visitor who has business with the husband. (2: 787)

Certainly Wharton's description of the Boynes' arrival in England and their subsequent rental of a country place with a ghost that nobody recognizes until "long long afterward" (2: 153) is, as Lewis points out, a promising beginning: the reader's curiosity is piqued by this tantalizing opener. At the same time, however, Wharton's belabored account of what is happening in the consciousness of her protagonist as she agonizes over her husband's sudden mysterious disappearance is a bit melodramatic. Nonetheless, aside from this weakness, Wharton does fashion a solid narrative. Her realistic portrayal of Mary Boyne and the "perfectly ordinary surroundings" does lend a "remarkable substantiality" to the tale, as Robillard suggests. More-over, the darkened downs, "the layers and layers of velvet shadow" (2: 155), and the "old dusky walls" (2: 172) of Lyng, the Boynes' English country house, provide just the right setting for a ghost to manifest itself. And, most important, Wharton avoids "the least touch of irrelevance, the least chill of inattention" (*WF* 38) in her gripping narrative.

The tale features the requisite preliminary horror—the grey figure of a man—and a telling sign-post—Ned's "shadow of anxiety, of perplexity" (2: 157), and, as is her wont, Wharton harps on these "horrors" throughout the tale. The fearsome "shadow of anxiety," in particular, serves two functions for Wharton: it is a suspenseful device—the reader wonders what is troubling the young writer—and it effects her protagonist's imprisonment with fear. Whenever Mary sees Ned's anxious face, her fear builds until, at tale's end, it completely overtakes her.

Again, it should be stressed that, unlike her early ghost story, Wharton reveals much of what is happening in Mary's consciousness with techniques characteristic of her late period—time shifts and interior monologues. The frequent juxtaposition of past and present, coupled with Wharton's entering the consciousness of her protagonist, enables the reader to witness firsthand Mary's growing imprisonment with fear.

The tale opens with the memorable line, "Oh, there *is* one, of course, but you'll never know it" (2: 152). Mary Boyne, sitting in the library of Lyng, an old English country house, on a cold December evening, reflects on the happy occasion when she first heard these words and on the events that followed this strange revelation. She remembers that she and her husband, "two romantic Americans" (2: 152), arrived in England six months before so that he could write a book on the "Economic Basis of Culture" and she could paint and garden. Originally a New Yorker, Mary had been exiled to Waukesha, a "soul-deadening" (2: 154) town in the Midwest where Ned was an engineer, until an unexpected windfall enabled them to retreat to this secluded English estate. She recalls that when their cousin, Alida Stair, revealed that Lyng had a ghost, they were even more delighted. "I don't want to have to drive ten miles to see somebody else's ghost," Ned insisted, "I want one of my own on the premises" (2: 153). Significantly, Mary also remembers being informed that they would not know of the ghost's presence until "long long afterward." Thus Wharton launches her narrative on the "note of inevitableness" that she favors at the beginning of her tales: "From the first I know exactly what is going to happen to every one of them; their [her characters'] fate is settled beyond rescue, and I have but to watch and record" (*BG* 204).

As Mary sits in the "shadows of the hearth" (2: 154) looking out on the downs "darkened to a deeper solitude" (2: 153–54), a silent setting designed to evoke the appearance of a ghostly visitant, she ponders her life at Lyng. She has not been as happy as she had hoped. She is especially disturbed by what she perceives as a strangeness in her husband. The recent "shadow of anxiety" (2: 157) appearing on his face—Wharton's telling sign-post—has led her to conclude that there is some secret he is keeping from her. Although she intuits that the secret is connected to their haunted house—he may have seen the ghost and is worried about what the specter revealed—she is deeply troubled that he has not confided the reason for his distress.

Immediately Wharton shifts to the past as Mary recalls when her husband's strange behavior began. She remembers that the previous October, when sharing a view from the roof, they spotted a youngish stranger in "loose greyish clothes" (2: 157) in "the grey-walled court" (2: 156) below. Deeply disturbed by the appearance of this man, Ned raced down the stairs to speak with him, but he had already disappeared. And her husband seemed relieved. For her part, Mary recollects only that her "shortsighted eyes" provided only "a blurred impression of slightness and greyishness" (2: 157), and she dismissed the incident as trivial. Wharton labels her eyes "shortsighted"—eye symbolism is very much in evidence in this tale—to suggest her protagonist's lack of foresight with respect to the disturbing incident: she failed to question the identity of the young man, and she neglected to investigate her husband's troubled reaction to his sudden appearance.

Now, as she looks out the library window and sees "a mere blot of deeper grey in the greyness" (2: 158), her husband's mysterious behavior and perplexed look disturb her anew. At first she identifies the figure as the Lyng ghost she and Ned were warned about, then as the grey figure they had seen from the roof. Unnerved by "the impending fear of the disclosure" (2: 158), her heart thumps—movements of the heart play a major role in signaling fear in this tale—until she is able to recognize that the approaching figure is her husband. Her fear dissipates—but not for long.

When she asks whether he is still trying to see the ghost, she detects again "the sharp stamp of worry between his brows" (2: 159), and her beating heart reflects her renewed fear. Although he responds that he has never tried, she is not convinced. She has not forgotten Alida Stair's warning that even when one sees a ghost, "one can't be sure till so long afterward" (2: 159).

At this point in the narrative, Wharton makes use of a letter—a familiar device—to effect a transformation in Ned Boyne. As soon as he receives it, Mary notices that "the lines of tension had vanished, and such traces of fatigue as lingered were of the kind easily attributable to steady mental effort" (2: 160). The same mail brings her a newspaper article about her husband: a man named Elwell claims that Ned cheated him in a mining transaction and has filed a lawsuit. Filled with "undefinable terror," she confronts her husband, whose face, when he perceives her distress, is once again darkened by the fearsome "shadow of apprehension" (2: 160). However, when he learns why she is so frightened, the shadow fades. With smiling eyes, he informs her that he has just received word that the lawsuit has been withdrawn. But Mary is not so easily comforted. She bemoans her lack of attention to her husband's "professional interests" and wonders "if she had done right" knowing so little of his "immediate preoccupations" (2: 161).

Wharton now skips ahead to the following morning. Mary remembers that her husband was no longer troubled, and she, too, felt a sense of relief. As she walked in the garden, "the espaliered pear trees," the fluttering pigeons, the "grass terrace," "the fish pond and yew hedges" mirrored how pleased she was with everything about the "sweet still place" (2: 163). Once again, Wharton employs a natural setting to reflect the mood of her central character. Only the "twisted chimney stacks and blue roof angles" suggest how ill-conceived "her recovered sense of safety" (2: 163) actually was.

Mary also recalls the youngish stranger with a wide-brimmed hat who disturbed her reverie that morning. He asked to see Mr. Boyne, but only after he indicated that he had come "a long way" (2: 164) did she lead him to her husband. She remembers, too, that the house was "so silent" (2: 164)—an appropriate setting for Wharton's ghost to appear—that she postponed interrupting her husband's writing. Even on discovering that he had left the house with a gentleman, she recalls experiencing only "a first faint tinge of disquietude" (2: 166).

Later in the day, however, when he still did not return, she was overcome "by a vague dread of the unknown" (2: 167). With "shortsighted eyes" (2: 167)—a phrase Wharton used ironically earlier in the tale to describe her protagonist when she viewed the shadowy stranger for the first time—she questioned the servants, and when the maid finally remembered that the gentleman wore a wide-brimmed hat, Mary realized with fright that it was she who had let him in to see her husband.

Back in the present, Mary acknowledges that there has been no word from her husband since his disappearance two weeks before. Only an unfinished letter to a Waukesha lawyer named Parvis has been discovered: "I have just received your letter announcing Elwell's death, and while I suppose there is now no further risk of trouble, it might be safer—" (2: 168). With hope waning that her husband will return, her consciousness experiences a

> lowering of velocity. . . . There were even moments of weariness when, like the victim of some poison which leaves the brain clear, but holds the body motionless, she saw herself domesticated with the Horror, accepting its perpetual presence as one of the fixed conditions of life. (2: 171)

Wharton capitalizes the word "horror" to emphasize the intensity of Mary's distress following Ned's disappearance. She also exploits images of enclosure—the house image, in particular—as her protagonist agonizes over her husband's whereabouts. Mary is certain "the house *knew*; the library in which she spent her long lonely evenings knew" (2: 171–72). And like

Paulina Anson in "The Angel at the Grave," she also senses that "the intense consciousness of the old dusty walls seemed about to break out into some audible revelation of their secret" (2: 172).

But the only revelations Mary receives are those from Parvis. He tells her that her husband bilked an associate, Bob Elwell, out of a fortune in a mining transaction; as a consequence, Elwell shot himself and subsequently died. His shocking allegations horrify Mary: she sits "motionless, her arms stretched along her knees in an attitude of rigid tension" (2: 173). To provide evidence for his story, Parvis shows her a newspaper account of the tragedy that contains photographs of Elwell and her husband. With "her heart hammering in her ears" (2: 174), Mary recognizes Elwell as the stranger who came to see her husband the day he disappeared. Further questioning reveals "the profoundest horror" (2: 175): Elwell shot himself on the day his ghost first appeared at Lyng and died the day before her husband disappeared.

Dumbstruck from the realization that it was the ghost of Elwell who spirited her husband away, Mary loses consciousness as the tale concludes: "she was numb to his touch, she did not know what he was saying" (2: 176). But she can still hear the clear voice of Alida Stair speaking: "You won't know till afterward . . . You won't know till long, long afterward" (2: 176).

Unlike Hartley in "The Lady's Maid's Bell" and Lady Jane in "Mr. Jones," Mary Boyne never confronts her ghost—the specter that has come between her and her husband. Although she fears that Ned is keeping something from her from the moment they arrive at Lyng, that there is in him an "undefinable change" that makes her "restless" and at times "tongue-tied" (2: 155), she questions him only when she receives the newspaper article implicating him in a lawsuit. When he assures her that everything has been settled, she dismisses her feelings of anxiety and too quickly experiences a sense of relief. In effect, she never examines the reasons for her faltering relationship with her husband. Consequently, after he is spirited away, she remains imprisoned with fearful knowledge of her painful short-comings.

"Pomegranate Seed" (1935), one of Wharton's last ghost stories (only "Old Souls' " followed it), is the final tale to be discussed in this study. Like "The Lamp of Psyche," the first story examined, this narrative is based on a Greek myth, that of Persephone. Clearly, Wharton's penchant for classical allusion continued to the end of her short story writing. Lewis labels "Pomegranate Seed" a "first-class ghost story" (495) and summarizes the classical myth:

Persephone, daughter of Demeter, goddess of fertility, was abducted and taken to Hades by Pluto, the god of the underworld. Her mother begged Jupiter to intercede, and he did so. But Persephone had broken her vow of abstinence in Hades by eating some pomegranate seeds. She was therefore required to spend a certain number of months each year—essentially the winter months—with Pluto. (2: 763n)

In Wharton's tale, an American couple, Charlotte and Kenneth Ashby, lead an idyllic existence until the ghost of Kenneth's first wife begins sending him letters—as soon as he and her successor return from their honeymoon—and, like Pluto in the Greek tale, comes to take him with her.

Although setting does not play as prominent a role in this later narrative as it does in "Afterward," the Ashbys' secluded library, "full of books and pipes and worn armchairs inviting to meditation" (2: 763), is not unlike the quiet library of the English country house "full of secrets . . . like the layers and layers of velvet shadow dropping from the low ceiling, the rows of books, the smoke-blurred sculpture of the hearth" (2: 155). Similarly, Wharton introduces a "preliminary horror" at the beginning of the tale—a mysterious gray envelope—that, like the grey figure in "Afterward," is mentioned repeatedly throughout the narrative. As McDowell points out, "Mrs. Wharton often made use of a single obsessive and obtrusive image to organize a given tale" ("Ghost Stories" 137). Of course, the unexplained appearance of the gray envelopes—nine in all—accounts for the mounting fear that imprisons Wharton's central character. Like Mary Boyne, she feels that "her husband was being dragged away from her into some mysterious bondage" (2: 777).

As the narrative begins, Charlotte Ashby, Wharton's protagonist, returns to the "veiled sanctuary" on a deserted street away from "the soulless roar of New York" (2: 763) that she and her husband of a little more than a year call home. From the outset images of imprisonment appear, as the omniscient narrator describes Charlotte's inserting her key into the lock of the quiet house with its "sash curtains drawn across the panes" (2: 763). The image of the drawn curtains blurring the light so that "no details showed" (2: 763) is not only a striking image of enclosure, it also foreshadows the end of the tale when Charlotte's sight becomes so blurred that she is unable to read the "details" of the mysterious ninth letter her missing husband has received.

Wharton also establishes suspense in the first section of her tale. The reader learns that Charlotte must force herself to enter the house: she is afraid that she will find another letter like the seven her husband has already received. Each one has been delivered by hand—there is neither stamp nor address—and each has appeared in a gray envelope with "visibly feminine" (2: 764) writing. The invisible sender of the envelopes provides the preliminary horror of the tale, and Wharton harps on this image throughout the narrative to sustain "the spell" (*WF* 38).

Charlotte reflects on the letters in the gray envelopes and the effect they have had on her relationship with her husband. In an interior monologue that occupies almost one-third of the narrative, Wharton attempts to "note down every half-aware stirring of thought and sensation, the automatic reactions to every passing impression" (*WF* 12) her protagonist experiences. She remembers that the first arrived the day after she and Kenneth returned from their honeymoon. Others followed, but Charlotte simply theorized that they were from a "tiresome client" or an "old entanglement" (2: 766). She had already been warned of his first wife's lingering hold on him before her marriage: "Whatever you venture to do, he'll mentally compare with what Elsie would have done in your place" (2: 766). But Kenneth has been "tender and lover-like" (2: 766) since their marriage. In fact, he has made her feel like "the sovereign even of his past" (2: 767).

However, of late, whenever he receives one of these letters, he wishes to be alone, "emptied of life and courage, and hardly conscious of her presence . . . far away from ordinary events" (2: 765). Consequently, every time she opens the door, she is filled with "a nervous apprehension" (2: 767), fearful a letter from the unknown woman will be there.

With the discovery of another letter on the hall table, Charlotte becomes so distraught that she decides to spy on her husband when he reads this latest missive. She sees him kiss the letter, and with her heart "beating excitedly" (2: 770)—once again Wharton's heart imagery signals the intensity of her protagonist's fear—she confronts him with what she has witnessed. Turning on her with "a face of terror and distress" (2: 771)—a sign-post that closely parallels that of the earlier "Afterward"—he admits that the letters are from a woman but insists that they are "about business," and "professional secrecy" (2: 770) prevents his divulging their contents. Fearful that she is being "excluded, ignored, blotted out of his life" (2: 772), Charlotte threatens to uncover the identity of the letter-writer even if it means she will lose his love.

Instead, she proposes that they take a holiday cruise. When he claims that it is impossible for him to get away, she points out that it was not impossible for him to take a two-month honeymoon. His elliptic reply—"at that time I didn't realize—" (2: 776) suggests to the reader, and perhaps to Charlotte as well, the identity of the letter-writer. Declaring "I can't leave—I can't" (2: 777), he breaks down and weeps. Charlotte becomes so frightened at the sight of her husband's distress that she resolves to "use up her last atom of strength in the struggle for his freedom, and for hers" (2: 777). She asks whether his mysterious letter-writer is forbidding him to leave. Obviously confused, he does not answer her question, but instead impulsively draws her to him and acquiesces to her request for an extended holiday: "Of course we'll go away together. We'll go wherever you want" (2: 778).

Charlotte's fear dissipates for a time. She feels relieved and victorious, no longer helpless. Now she will be able "to release him from the evil spell he was under" (2: 779). She sings because she feels she has scored a "victory" (2: 779). In this narrative, Wharton repeats the word "victory" in much the same way that she repeats "not till long long afterward" in "Afterward": both signal a false sense of security. Indeed, Charlotte is so ecstatic that she experiences only "a faint shiver of apprehension" (2: 780) when she calls Kenneth's office and discovers that he has gone out of town. Although she believes he may be looking for permission from the mysterious letter-writer to take their extended holiday, she still feels she can "claim the victory" (2: 780).

However, as the hours pass and there is no word from her husband, the fear that earlier overwhelmed her reappears. Aware that "her nervousness [is] gaining on her" (2: 782), she visits her mother-in-law to discuss her husband's day-long absence. Together they return to the Ashbys' "quiet house" only to find another gray envelope on the hall table. No longer willing to keep "the premonition of something inexplicable, intolerable" (2: 767) concealed, Charlotte, her heart beating "excitedly" (2: 783), asks her mother-in-law if she recognizes the handwriting. Mrs. Ashby pales and her hand shakes—familiar physical characteristics signaling extreme emotional distress in Wharton's tales—as she admits that the writing on the letter belongs to Kenneth's first wife. Her daughter-in-law confesses she suspected that was the case.

Then, with trembling hands that reveal her overpowering fear of touching "the little personal effects of someone newly dead" (2: 785), she slits open the envelope. Her eyes blur as she strains to read the writing, which is faint and illegible. Wharton describes Charlotte's repeated efforts to read the letter; however, to evoke the "fear, simple shivering animal fear," that will grab her reader "by the throat" (WF 41), she opts to leave the letter unread. Her sight "blurred," Charlotte is only able to make out the words "mine" and "come" (2: 786)—even with the help of a magnifying glass.

As the tale concludes, Charlotte, exhausted from her bout with overpowering fear, realizes that it is the ghost of her husband's first wife who is finally victorious: "Don't you see that she's everywhere in this house, and the closer to him because to everyone else she's become invisible?" (2: 787). Like Pluto in the Greek myth, Elsie has abducted Kenneth and restored his fidelity to her. And like Mary Boyne, who "was sure that Boyne would never come back" (2: 171), Wharton's protagonist knows it will not "do any good to do anything" (2: 788). Charlotte, like Mary, failed to confront her ghost: she waited helplessly until her husband received his eighth letter before questioning him about the sender. Of course, his disappearance leaves her hopelessly disconsolate: she is certain she has lost him forever.

Here again, parallels can be drawn in the story line and theme of "Pomegranate Seed" and "Afterward," the tale with which it is paired. Both tell of wives terrified by their husband's strange behavior and disappearance with a ghost. Both conclude as each wife becomes aware of the reason behind her husband's disappearance. Sadly, in both tales, Wharton's protagonists are left imprisoned with fear, paralyzed by the realization that "Death itself had waited that day on the threshold" (2: 171).

Both tales also contain many of the same techniques. Wharton's spectral setting at Lyng, the "old house hidden under a shoulder of the downs" (2: 154) in "Afterward," has its counterpart in the closed shuttered house in New York hidden from "congested traffic" and "congested houses" (2: 763). Even Wharton's references to these houses at the conclusion of the tales are very much the same: in "Afterward," Mary acknowledges that only "the house *knew*" what had become of her husband, and in "Pomegranate Seed," Charlotte concludes, "The bare walls cry it [that a ghost exists] out" (2: 787). The revealing sign-posts are also remarkably similar. Ned's face is covered with "shadow of anxiety" each time the stranger appears, and Kenneth's face displays "terror and distress" (2: 771) each time the gray envelope is mentioned. The fluctuating peristalic action appears in both tales as well: both women are frightened by the troubled faces of their husbands, pacified by their assurances, and horror-stricken after they disappear.

Perhaps the only difference in Wharton's technique in these tales involves the shape of the ghosts. In the earlier tale, Wharton's ghost appears—he is visible—much like the ghost of Emma Saxon in "The Lady's Maid's Bell." In "Pomegranate Seed," as in "Mr. Jones," the ghost does not appear: "She's become invisible" (2: 787), Charlotte wails. Perhaps, in her desire to fashion "a good ghost" (*WF* 39), Wharton determined that a ghost that is imperceptible is more exciting, more suspenseful, more frightening—which is, as she points out in *The Writing of Fiction*, "what writers of ghost stories are after" (41).

In her discussion of the ghost story in *The Writing of Fiction*, Edith Wharton points out, "One of the chief obligations, in a short story, is to give the reader an immediate sense of security" (37). In her tales of the supernatural, Wharton does just that. She does not mislead. She provides telling sign-posts—often a physical characteristic—designed to "make" her reader believe in ghosts. Alice Hartley's "turn[ing] cold" (1: 465) when she hears footsteps coming from the locked room in "The Lady's Maid's Bell," Lady Jane's "inward shiver" (2: 610–11) as she crosses the threshold of the blue parlor in "Mr. Jones," Mary Boyne's "look of terror" (2: 173) when she asks about the greyish figure in the courtyard in "Afterward," and Charlotte Ashby's "premonitory chill" (2: 767) each time she catches sight of another mysterious gray letter in "Pomegranate Seed" are such sign-posts.

Of course, from her earliest tale, "The Lady's Maid's Bell," with the "very still night" (1: 472), to one of her last, "Pomegranate Seed," with the "quiet house" (2: 763) on a deserted street, all of Wharton's narratives contain the silence and continuity required for ghosts "to make themselves manifest" (2: 876). Likewise, in each tale, Wharton posits a preliminary horror—usually a strange figure—and she harps on this image to help send a cold shiver down her reader's spine. Most important, Wharton introduces a unique kind of peristaltic action in each of her ghost stories. Alternating waves of fear and calm parallel the mysterious occurrences and quiet moments in the narrative. Ultimately, these alternations presage a tragedy and reveal an "inescapable symbolic truth." In Wharton's early "The Lady's Maid's Bell," the alternations are abrupt and well defined, with each period of quiet climaxed by the conjuring up of a ghost. In her later tales, the alternations are more subtle: the ghosts do not always appear as suddenly, nor are they as recognizable. In fact, the final apparition is often obscure and fleeting—hence, the intense fear paralyzing Wharton's imprisoned protagonists.

Wharton's technical artistry also evidences several developments in her later ghost stories. Images of imprisonment proliferate in her vivid description of setting and in her portrayal of character. The dialogue is often overrun with references to keys, locks, and forbidden rooms. Finally, Wharton graphically records her protagonists' every movement and physical reaction: all of their fearful shivers, jerking heartbeats, and inward chills are carefully recorded so that the reader will know the intensity of the fear experienced by these imprisoned victims.

Wharton does, therefore, observe her requirements for a good ghost story. As McDowell points out:

Edith Wharton's ghost stories represent, in general, the work of a mature and sophisticated artist. These works form a well-defined group in subject and technique, and they provide a convenient focus for an inquiry into Mrs. Wharton's methods and achievements in short fiction. Like the best of her other efforts in this genre, the short stories of the macabre and the supernatural, more often than not, manifest in concentrated fashion the careful technique, the evocative style, and the concern for aesthetic order that she revealed in her best novels. ("Ghost Stories" 133)

Chapter Six

Conclusion: Wharton's Thematic and Technical Development from Her Early to Her Later Tales

R.W.B. Lewis, in the introduction to his two-volume edition of Edith Wharton's short stories, begins by pointing out that "Edith Wharton began as a writer of short stories, and, in a sense, she finished as one" (vii). Nonetheless, up to the present time, Wharton's eleven volumes of eighty-six tales have received relatively little critical attention. Even the revived interest in Wharton during the 1960s, the publication of Lewis's edition of her tales in 1968, and his more recent edition of her letters in 1988 have not resulted in an outpouring of criticism on her writing in this genre. Although a few of her tales have been anthologized and singled out for commentary, much of her short fiction has been ignored.

Perhaps this lack of attention is due in part to the unfavorable comments made by some critics regarding the subject matter of Wharton's short stories. Irving Howe, for example, mentions the "sense of fatality" in Wharton's fiction, the absence of a "vocabulary of happiness" (17–18), and H. Wayne Morgan notes: "The pessimism that was intensified by her old age was present in all her work. Of all modern major American writers, her view of mankind is perhaps the darkest" (35). Louis Kronenberger, one of the most outspoken reviewers of Lewis's two-volume work, finds her stories "readable," but claims that they

have rightly not counted much in the revival of her reputation: they can be astute and mature as well as trivial and merely entertaining, but they contrib-

ute nothing to the enlargement of literature, and they are almost never
literature themselves. What is literature or has a comparable value rests in
Mrs. Wharton's longer fiction. (99–100)

Blake Nevius also contends that "most of Edith Wharton's stories are so
slight in subject and execution that the exceptions stand out. She wrote
perhaps a dozen short stories good enough for any anthology, but she also
wrote more than her share of ephemera" (28–29).

Nonetheless, other critics comment more favorably on the content of
Wharton's tales. Margaret B. McDowell, for example, maintains that "her
best tales reveal extraordinary psychological and moral insight; and they
achieve distinction through her exploration in them of human situations of
considerable complexity" (*Wharton* 85). Similarly, Van Wyck Brooks
points out that "one had to fall back on her short stories to find Edith
Wharton at her best in connection with living people in the modern world"
(291).

Others praise Wharton's short story artistry, even finding it superior to
that in her novels. Grace Kellogg argues, for example, that "the short
medium was more congenial to her than the novel," that in the novel
Wharton "fumbled her way to mastery of her craft," but in the short story
"she was mistress of it from the start" (234–35). Kellogg's sentiments are
reiterated by Blanche Colton Williams, who notes, "In her novels her talent
has found exercise, through freer expression, to her greater popularity; in
her short stories, through a more restricted medium, to her perfection of art"
(337). Likewise, Fred Lewis Pattee asserts, "The *conte*, the modern short
story, is an art form: technique is its life-blood, and Mrs. Wharton first of
all is a craftsman" (253).

This study, therefore, has concentrated on the development of Wharton's
technical artistry, especially in relation to the subject that dominates her
short stories—the theme of imprisonment, of "prisoners of consciousness."
Tales from Wharton's early period have been compared to those of her major
and late periods having similar subject matter and story lines to demonstrate,
as Geoffrey Walton points out, that "Edith Wharton's form and style
underwent a very visible evolutionary process during her forty-odd years
of creative effort" (208–9). Moreover, most of the tales analyzed have had
little or no critical commentary and have been selected in order to show that
even those stories considered unworthy of attention are not, as Nevius
claims, "so slight in subject and execution." In each of them, Wharton
displays her thematic and technical achievement.

In the early tales examined in this study, Wharton employs a variety of
techniques to present her imprisonment theme. Because she believed that

"how to make a beginning" (*WF* 50) should be a writer's first concern, her early tales frequently have provocative openers. In "The Reckoning," for example, the opening line, "The marriage law of the new dispensation will be: *'Thou shalt not be unfaithful—to thyself,'* " captures the reader's attention and provides valuable clues as to the cause and extent of the imprisonment that Julia Westall, her disconsolate protagonist, endures.

Similarly, words that "tell" and phrases that act as sign-posts punctuate Wharton's early narratives. Q. D. Leavis points out that "her real strength lay in the critical phrases she uses" (207–8), and in "The Line of Least Resistance," the critical phrase, "late—as usual" provides a striking example. This opener epitomizes the predicament of Mindon, Wharton's imprisoned central character (who discovers that it is too late for him to escape his marital prison), and furnishes a thematic sign-post for the entire tale.

Symbolic settings, which Wharton defines as "event[s] in the history of a soul" (*WF* 85), can also be found in these early narratives to mirror her protagonists' feelings of imprisonment. In her first tale, "Mrs. Manstey's View," she introduces the image of the enclosed space—the third floor back room of a New York boardinghouse—to symbolize the "condition in life" (Lewis 121) of an isolated elderly widow. And she makes use of the house and its different rooms to dramatize the locked-in existence of her central characters in many of the tales that follow.

Most important, in these early tales, Wharton relies on dramatic irony and sophisticated satire—stylistic devices for which she is especially distinguished—to highlight her imprisonment theme. Irony dominates the story lines of both "The Lamp of Psyche" and "The Reckoning," where she portrays wives entrapped in marital dilemmas that are ironically of their own making: in effect, they are responsible for imprisoning themselves. Likewise, satire plays a major role in such early tales as "A Cup of Cold Water" and "The Recovery," where Wharton levels stinging attacks on the artificial, vacuous upper-class society that wields such devastating control over her vulnerable heroes and heroines.

Wharton also experiments with a number of other techniques in her early tales. The eye imagery characteristic of all her fiction—"beginning with physique, she [Wharton] is particularly interested in eyes" (Russell, "Imagery" 457)—appears as early as 1895 in "The Lamp of Psyche" to mirror the inner thoughts of a newly married woman. She interjects a tale-within-a-tale in "A Cup of Cold Water" to effect a transformation in a deeply troubled embezzler, and she plays with names in "Friends" to echo the entrapment of two presumably close school teacher friends. In "That Good May Come," she juxtaposes light and dark to highlight the choice between good and evil confronting a fledgling poet, and she relies on classical allusion, the myth of Cupid and Psyche, as the basis for the marital entrapment described in "The Lamp of Psyche."

Finally, in her first tale of the supernatural, "The Lady's Maid's Bell," Wharton introduces a number of unusual techniques in order to provide excitement and suspense. A preliminary horror, revealing sign-posts, and a kind of peristaltic action that climaxes in an *illuminating incident* (*WF* 109)—devices Wharton details at length in *The Writing of Fiction* and the Preface to *Ghosts*—engage and absorb the reader. She also makes use of the first-person point of view to increase the "immediacy and freshness" (Brooks and Warren 661) of the narrative and, of course, to heighten suspense. Although Wharton favors an omniscient narrator as the angle that will "give out all its [the story's] fires," occasionally (in about one-quarter of her tales), she shifts the angle to a first-person teller to ensure "the right one" (*WF* 48–49).

In her later tales, Wharton's imprisonment theme remains paramount, and many of the techniques employed in her early tales reappear, albeit more prominently than before. Irony, a mainstay of her early tales, for example, becomes more pervasive in Wharton's later narratives—boldly dramatic in "Permanent Wave," where an unfaithful wife realizes, during her four-hour imprisonment in the waver, that her monotonous existence with her boring husband is preferable to an uncertain future with an exciting explorer, and painfully tragic in "The Day of the Funeral," where an unfaithful husband discovers, after his wife's suicide, that his unresponsive spouse was, in reality, a passionate woman. Similarly, Wharton makes lavish use of satire in the later tales, in particular in her graphic representations of the lifestyle of the upper class. In "Duration" and "The Pretext," for example, her scathing satire enriches her descriptions of the societal pressures that occasion her central characters' locking themselves into different kinds of external control.

Not surprisingly, images of imprisonment—often subtle and indirect in the early tales—now become more numerous and more explicit. Many of the late tales, especially "The Bolted Door," "Afterward," "Mr. Jones," and "Pomegranate Seed," contain frequent allusions to locked doors, slipping bolts, closing gates, ticking clocks, closed shutters, and clinking chains.

A close examination of Wharton's later narratives reveals a variety of additional distinctive techniques. Imagery of the heart—as it leaps, pounds, drops, and contracts—and movements of the hands—as they twitch, shake, and become clammy—are added to imagery of the eyes to help reveal the innermost thoughts of her imprisoned protagonists. In "The Day of the Funeral," for example, the agitated hands of an adulterous university professor mirror his disturbed thoughts following his wife's suicide.

Wharton's use of language also contains marked changes in many of her later tales. Often the dialogue of her central characters signals not only the "culminating moments" (*WF* 73) of her early stories, but also "the significant passages of their talk" (*BG* 203). In "The Potboiler," for example, Wharton uses a series of exchanges between an idealistic impoverished artist and a wealthy picture dealer to highlight the societal pressures that hasten the apostasy of the young painter.

The framing device becomes more conspicuous. Wharton frames several of her late stories—in particular, "The Verdict" and "The Daunt Diana"—to present a "dramatic rendering of a situation" (*WF* 47) and to emphasize the static condition of her entrapped victims.

Furthermore, time shifts, most notably the flashback, are increasingly evident. In early tales like "The Lamp of Psyche," transformations in her characters are invariably swift and without explanation: Wharton does not reveal how these imprisoned individuals suddenly arrive at certain momentous decisions in their lives. In her later narratives, Wharton employs "excursions into the past" (Macauley and Lanning 155)—"The Letters" shines in this respect—to expose those events that catapulted her protagonists into their present entrapped state.

But perhaps the most crucial development in Wharton's later tales is the introduction of techniques that reveal the inner consciousness of her protagonists firsthand. Interior monologues that "imitate the associational flow of thought" (Wright 342) and record the "mental as well as visual reactions" of her protagonists "just as they come" (*WF* 12) appear with greater frequency in Wharton's later stories. This technique is decidedly more effective in developing the theme of imprisonment than the external descriptions of her early tales. In "The Bolted Door," for example, the reader is made fully aware of the agonizing deliberations occurring in the obsessed mind of an undiscovered murderer: Wharton enters his guilt-ridden consciousness to reveal the nature and extent of the imprisonment he endures.

It becomes clear, therefore, that life remains a prison for Wharton's entrapped victims of circumstance, and throughout her early, major, and late periods of storytelling, she sought, as E. K. Brown points out, "exactly [the] right mode of presenting a subject, the mode which would bring out every last iota of possibility the subject had" (68).

References

PRIMARY SOURCES

Wharton, Edith. *A Backward Glance.* New York: Scribner's, 1934.
_____. *The Collected Short Stories of Edith Wharton.* Edited by R.W.B. Lewis. 2 vols. New York: Scribner's, 1968.
_____. Letter to Judge Robert Grant, November 19, 1907. Beinecke Rare Book and Manuscript Library, Yale University, New Haven, Conn.
_____. Letter to Sara Norton, April 8, 1906. Beinecke Rare Book and Manuscript Library, Yale University, New Haven, Conn.
_____. *The Letters of Edith Wharton.* Edited by R.W.B. Lewis and Nancy Lewis. New York: Scribner's, 1988.
_____. *The Writing of Fiction.* New York: Scribner's, 1925. Reprint. New York: Octagon, 1966.

SECONDARY SOURCES

Beach, Joseph Warren. *The Twentieth Century Novel: Studies in Technique.* New York: Appleton, 1932.
Bewley, Marius. "Mrs. Wharton's Mask." In *Masks and Mirrors: Essays in Criticism.* New York: Atheneum, 1970. 145–53.
Blackall, Jean Frantz. "Wharton's Art of Ellipsis." Paper presented at the Edith Wharton Conference, Lenox, Mass., June 9, 1987.
Brooks, Cleanth, and Robert Penn Warren. *Understanding Fiction.* 2nd ed. New York: Appleton, 1959.

Brooks, Van Wyck. *The Confident Years: 1885–1915*. New York: Dutton, 1955.

Brown, E. K. "Edith Wharton." In *Edith Wharton: A Collection of Critical Essays*. Edited by Irving Howe. Englewood Cliffs: Prentice-Hall, 1962. 62–72.

Cooper, Frederick Taber. *Some American Story Tellers*. New York: Holt, 1911.

French, Marilyn. "The Emergence of Edith Wharton." *New Republic,* June 13, 1981, 25–31.

Hardwick, Elizabeth. "Mrs. Wharton in New York." *New York Review of Books*, January 21, 1988, 28–34.

Hicks, Granville. "The Intense Aristocrat." *Saturday Review*, August 3, 1968, 17–18.

Howe, Irving. "Introduction: The Achievement of Edith Wharton." In *Edith Wharton: A Collection of Critical Essays*. Edited by Irving Howe. Englewood Cliffs: Prentice-Hall, 1962. 1–18.

Kellogg, Grace. *The Two Lives of Edith Wharton: The Woman and Her Work*. New York: Appleton, 1965.

Kimbel, Ellen. "The American Short Story: 1900–1920." In *The American Short Story: 1900–1945*. Edited by Philip Stevick. Boston: Twayne, 1984. 33–69.

Kronenberger, Louis. "Mrs. Wharton's Literary Museum." *Atlantic Monthly* 222 (September 1968): 98–102.

Leavis, Q. D. "Henry James's Heiress: The Importance of Edith Wharton." In *Collected Essays: The American Novel and Reflections on the European Novel*. 2 vols. Edited by G. Singh. Cambridge Mass.: Cambridge University Press, 1985. 2: 194–208.

Lewis, R.W.B. *Edith Wharton: A Biography*. New York: Harper, 1975.

Lindberg, Gary H. *Edith Wharton and the Novel of Manners*. Charlottesville: University Press of Virginia, 1975.

Macauley, Robie, and George Lanning. *Technique in Fiction*. New York: Harper, 1964.

McDowell, Margaret B. *Edith Wharton*. Boston: Twayne, 1976.

———. "Edith Wharton's Ghost Stories." *Criticism* 12 (Spring 1970): 133–52.

Miller, James E. Jr. "Wharton and Cather: The Quest for Culture." In *Quests Surd and Absurd: Essays in American Literature*. Chicago: University of Chicago Press, 1967. 79–90.

Morgan, H. Wayne. *Writers in Transition: Seven Americans*. New York: Hill and Wang, 1963.

Nevius, Blake. *Edith Wharton: A Study of Her Fiction*. 1953. Reprint. Berkeley: University of California Press, 1961.

O'Faolain, Sean. *The Short Story*. New York: Devin-Adair, 1964.

Pattee, Fred Lewis. *The New American Literature 1890–1930*. New York: Century, 1930.

Plante, Patricia R. "Edith Wharton as Short Story Writer." *Midwest Quarterly* 4 (Summer 1963): 363–79.

Quinn, Arthur Hobson. *American Fiction: An Historical and Critical Survey.* New York: Appleton, 1936.

Robillard, Douglas. "Edith Wharton 1862–1937." In *Supernatural Fiction Writers: Fantasy and Horror.* 2 vols. Edited by Everett Franklin Bleiler. New York: Scribner's, 1985. 2: 783–88.

Russell, Frances Theresa. "Edith Wharton's Use of Imagery." *English Journal* 21 (1932): 452–61.

———. "Melodramatic Mrs. Wharton." *Sewanee Review* 40 (1932): 425–37.

Van Doren, Carl. *The American Novel.* Rev. ed. New York: Macmillan, 1946.

Walton, Geoffrey. *Edith Wharton: A Critical Interpretation.* 2nd ed. Rutherford, N.J.: Fairleigh Dickinson University Press, 1982.

White, Barbara A. *Edith Wharton: A Study of the Short Fiction.* New York: Twayne, 1991.

Williams, Blanche Colton. *Our Short Story Writers.* 1920. Reprint. Freeport, N.Y.: Books for Libraries, 1969.

Wilson, Edmund. "Justice to Edith Wharton." In *The Wound and the Bow: Seven Studies in Literature.* Boston: Houghton Mifflin, 1941. 195–213.

Wolff, Cynthia Griffin. *A Feast of Words: The Triumph of Edith Wharton.* New York: Oxford University Press, 1977.

Wright, Austin McGiffert. *The American Short Story in the Twenties.* Chicago: University of Chicago Press, 1961.

Zilversmit, Annette. "Edith Wharton's Last Ghosts." *College Literature* 14 (1987): 296–305.

Index

Hicks, Granville, 28
House imagery, 18–19, 31, 36, 88–
    92, 102, 107–8, 115–17, 119–20.
    See also Enclosure imagery
Howe, Irving, 38, 123

Illuminating incident, 6, 126
Imagery. *See* Enclosure imagery; Eye
    Imagery; Heart imagery; Hand im-
    agery; House imagery; Imprison-
    ment imagery; Light/dark imagery
Imprisonment imagery, 2–4, 13–14,
    16–17, 19–20, 23–24, 26, 29–32,
    36, 41–43, 45, 50–51, 53–56, 59–
    60, 62–64, 66, 72–75, 86, 89–92,
    95, 102, 104, 107–9, 117, 125–26
Imprisonment, theme of, 2–4
Interior monologue, 17, 20, 25, 32,
    47, 53–54, 56, 58, 62, 66, 77, 88,
    118, 127
Irony, 13, 15–17, 21, 24, 27–28, 31–
    32, 34–35, 43–49, 52–53, 55–58,
    62, 65–66, 74, 77–81, 83–84, 88,
    91, 102, 109, 125–26

"Joy in the House," stream of con-
    sciousness in, 8

Kellogg, Grace, 124
Kimbel, Ellen, 22
Kronenberger, Louis, 123

"Lady's Maid's Bell, The": general
    discussion, 102–6; narrative tech-
    niques, 102, 121, 125; compared
    to "Mr. Jones," 111–112; first-per-
    son teller, 102; heart imagery,
    105; house imagery, 102; impris-
    onment imagery, 102, 104; irony,
    102; peristaltic action, 102–6, 126;
    preliminary horror, 100, 102–3;
    sign-post, 102–4, 106; symbolic
    setting, 102, 105

"Lamp of Psyche, The": general dis-
    cussion, 13–16; narrative tech-
    niques, 12–13; compared to "The
    Letters," 20–21; classical allusion,
    13–14, 16, 126; eye imagery, 14,
    125; face imagery, 15; hasty trans-
    formation, 16, 127; imprisonment
    imagery, 3, 13–14, 16; irony, 13,
    15, 125; satire, 13–15; symbolic
    settings, 13–14
Leavis, Q. D., 125
"Letters, The": general discussion,
    16–20; narrative techniques, 12,
    16–17, 38; compared to "The
    Lamp of Psyche," 20–21; dia-
    logue, 18–19; eye imagery, 18;
    flashbacks, 17, 20–21, 127; heart
    imagery, 17–20; house imagery,
    18–19; imprisonment imagery, 17,
    19–20; interior monologues, 17,
    20; irony, 16–17; symbolic set-
    tings, 19
Lewis, R.W.B., *Biography of Edith
    Wharton, The*, 2, 9, 12, 18, 21, 33,
    51–52, 62, 73–74, 106, 112, 116–
    17, 125; *Collected Short Stories of
    Edith Wharton, The*, 60, 117, 123;
    Letters of Edith Wharton, The, 1
Light/dark imagery, 71, 73, 125
Lindberg, Gary H., 2, 107–8
"Line of Least Resistance, The": gen-
    eral discussion, 21–24; narrative
    techniques, 12, 21, 37; compared
    to "Permanent Wave," 27–28; dra-
    matic opening, 21, 125; enclosure
    imagery, 23; hasty transformation,
    23; imprisonment imagery, 23–24;
    irony, 21, 24; satire, 21–22; sym-
    bolic settings, 22–24; time im-
    agery, 21, 23–24
Love and marriage stories: general
    discussion, 11; narrative tech-
    niques, 12, 37–38

Temps . . . ," 3; "Bolted Door,
The," 3–4, 40, 52–58, 126–27;
"Confession," 4; "Cup of Cold
Water, A," 39–40, 47–52, 57–58,
67, 125; "Daunt Diana, The," 70,
93–98, 127; "Day of the Funeral,
The," 4, 12, 32–37, 126; "Duration," 7, 40, 44–47, 126;
"Friends," 7, 39–40, 58–62, 66–
67, 125; "Joy in the House," 8;
"Lady's Maid's Bell, The," 100,
102–6, 111–12, 121, 125; "Lamp
of Psyche, The," 3, 12–16, 20–21,
125–27; "Letters, The," 12, 16–
21, 38, 127; "Line of Least Resistance, The," 12, 21–24, 27–28, 37,
125; "Moving Finger, The," 8;
"Mr. Jones," 100, 106–12, 121,
126; "Mrs. Manstey's View," 2–3,
39–44, 46–47, 67, 125; "Permanent Wave," 6, 12, 24–28, 38,
126; "Pomegranate Seed," 100,
116–21, 126; "Potboiler, The," 6,
70, 75–79, 97, 127; "Pretext,
The," 40, 62–67, 126; "Reckoning, The," 12, 28–32, 36–37, 125;
"Recovery, The," 70, 79–84, 87–
88, 125; "Seed of Faith, The," 6;
"That Good May Come," 3, 70–
74, 78–79, 97, 125; "Triumph of
Night, The," 3; "Verdict, The,"
70, 84–88, 97, 127

Wharton, Edward (Teddy), 4
White, Barbara A., 104
Williams, Blanche Colton, 124
Wilson, Edmund, 68
Wolff, Cynthia Griffin, 12, 37, 40–41
Wright, Austin McGiffert, 127

Zilversmit, Annette, 101

About the Author

EVELYN E. FRACASSO is Professor of English at Quinnipiac College in Hamden, Connecticut. She is the author of articles on Edith Wharton, Willa Cather, Joan Didion, and William Faulkner.